To John T. —

The Offbeat Angler

A Brown Water Boys Adventure

FLAT HAMMOCK PRESS
MYSTIC, CONNECTICUT

Flat Hammock Press
5 Church Street
Mystic, Connecticut 06355
860.572.2722
www.flathammockpress.com

Library of Congress Cataloging-in-Publication Data

Arelt, Christopher.
   The offbeat angler / by Christopher Arelt, Sebastian O'Kelly.
      p. cm.
ISBN 0-9718303-5-5
   1. Fishing--Anecdotes. I. O'Kelly, Sebastian. II. Title.
SH441.A667 2004
799.12--dc22
                        2003023739

ISBN 0-9718303-5-5

Offbeat Angler – Concept and Name: Christopher Arelt
Fishing Expedition Leader – Concept and Design: Sebastian O'Kelly
Fishing Puns – Sebastian O'Kelly
Brown Water Boys – Concept and Name: Christopher Arelt
Writer of Most and Tallest Fish Tales – Sebastian O'Kelly
Cover Concept – Christopher Arelt
Illustrations – Christopher Arelt
Mulberry Fly Originator – Sebastian O'Kelly

Cover Design – Cummings and Good
Interior Layout and Design – Stewart Jordan

Printed in the United States of America

First printing:
10 9 8 7 6 5 4 3 2 1

To Elizabeth

To Mother Nature, may she endure the ravages of Man

Contents

Acknowledgments

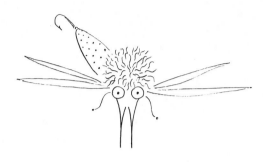

We would like to thank the following individuals for their contributions to the book: Patrick O'Kelly for aiding and abetting the addiction at an early age; Mdsdo for recognizing the writing potential early on; Shultzie for feedback on early chapters; Stewart Jordan for sorting out the guts of the work; Norm Shaw for guidance at a critical juncture; Jimmy Koplow for advice on the nuances of publishing; also, Ricky Aitken, Chris Beukers, Scott Holroyd, Rob Nasser, Tom Schoendorf, Walt Tramposch, and Andy Ulrich; last but not least, the Fishing God for blessing our lines.

Introduction

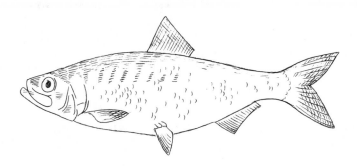

The Brown Water Boys are pleased to bring you this offbeat collection of fish tales from our muddy adventures. Since a young age both of us, Sebastian and Christopher, have, you might say, taken the river less traveled. Getting chased off Old Man Johnson's farm pond was just the beginning but offered an early glimpse into our fishing future. Over the years, independently and in tandem, we have found ourselves in all manner of unusual circumstances: skidding down a gravel escarpment, tackle boxes flying, as we headed for a hard-to-reach oasis; sneaking past a stately mansion en route to an early morning appointment with oversized treats at a hidden pond; braving the foulest weather to wet our lines in an oily ditch. Only recently did we come to realize, upon reflection, that our angling activities tend to fall outside the norm; at which point we resolved to embrace rather than conceal our uniqueness, proclaim the virtues of such iconoclasm to the world, and consciously and aggressively scan the periphery for even more extreme renditions to bring under our brand. Permit us to give you a sampling of what's inside.

Some might classify fishing in reservoir spillways and nuclear plant outflows as not just offbeat but downright dangerous. Though when you hear about fish after fish being caught, albeit some with a Chernobyl tan, you may want to lift your objection. Chasing aquarium rejects from an abandoned tropical fish collection in a big city canal—that sounds bizarre. But maybe less so when you find out that the King of All Gamefish hangs in the same place. As for monkey fishing...these people must be lunatics!

Perhaps. This is also not one of those "how to" fishing books offering instruction on the precise angle of one's arm for the perfect backcast. Oh, you will learn a tactical trick or two. Like how to tie a "berry" fly to fool streetwise, trashcan-sized carp. Sneak a cast between the maws of giant front-end loaders. Respond to queries from strangers when walking through the city wearing a suit, with a strung-up fly rod in one hand and a briefcase in the other. These advanced maneuvers are not for amateurs.

You'll meet some interesting characters, in print and through a bevy of Christopher's illustrations. Tap your foot to Fish Rapper's #1 album, *Throwin' Da Loop Da Loop*. Meet all the happening people at THE summer event as the ultra-smooth Perry Fontaine unveils his historic fly fishing collection. Cackle at the antics of Mullet Man and Fly Girl on the famed Buffalo Ford in Yellowstone National Park. Hold on to your seat as the Land Captain reveals his suicidal tendencies while jamming eighty-five down Alligator Alley. Grin at those two old fops, Sir Chalmers Castworthy and Godfrey Lightibbets Esq., as they debate the virtues of fishing a waste-ridden Superfund site. Sounds like fiction? We do have a fable or two to tell—what good fishing story doesn't—plus a poem and an ample creel full of bad fishing puns. But most of the stories and characters are true-to-life. Honest.

It may look like chaotic madness but offbeat angling does have a philosophy behind it. It's not easy to define but, for better or worse, a disdain for authority and "fishing conformism" are recurring themes. There's an interest in fishing backwaters and byways that many turn their noses up at as they jet to the latest glory spot. A willingness to embrace a variety of fishing gear and techniques, though for the sake of fairness, challenge and legality we avoid some—like dynamite. A rejection of the human impulse to assign social status to fish species—except the bait-nabbing rock bass. A recognition that urban, seemingly polluted waters ignored by all, save the municipal sewage treatment plant, can bear fruit. Fly fishing, spin fishing, bait fishing—there's room on the bank for all tastes in our world.

We don't cast tradition completely aside. After all, an offbeat-only approach can create its own type of conformism. Rather, we are interested in catching fish by hook *or* by hackle, focusing on the quality of each event, considering what limiting factors may exist at the time. In the end, it's about fun, friends and fishing, with more than a few laughs along the way. It's undeniable that there's a lot of enthusiasm here, and we hope it's infectious enough for others to join in. There's a little offbeat angler and brown water fisherman in us all. With the human population, development and global warming on the rise, our approach may well become the wave of the future.

But don't expect to see fishermen shoulder-to-shoulder along an I-95 highway ditch anytime soon.

The Formative Years

By Christopher Arelt

Although Sebastian and I are convinced that a little Brown Water Boy lies within every fisherman, I myself was destined for this course from the beginning. My earliest fishing trips were made with my best friend in the second grade, Ricky Aitken. We were chaperoned by Ricky's mother, herself a fisherwoman, and we usually ended up at a local pier or floating dock, fishing for flounder or snapper blues. I firmly believe that a positive first experience is the foundation of a long, happy relationship with our beloved pastime, whatever one's age at the time. If you get skunked, chances are you come away thinking that fishing is pointless, a colossal waste of time. You make a mental note never to fish again. But if you catch something, even have some nibbles, you'll probably be hooked for life. I certainly was when I pulled up a doormat (probably more like a mousepad) on my very first try.

Soon we were old enough to bike to our fishing holes, which had expanded to include some local ponds and a few more remote salt-water spots. We explored the shores, looking for bait as we went, finding our own way and a good deal of mischief. I'm not sure mischief is part and parcel of offbeat angling. It's probably more related to what made life interesting for me personally in those days. Still, mischief tends to spice up an otherwise unsuccessful outing as one's affinity for fishing itself is developing, so in that regard it's a valuable, though not essential, ingredient. Between the ages of seven and fourteen, I had any number of willing accomplices (names have been changed to protect the not-so-innocent).

On Saturday mornings we headed to the twin ponds, so named because they were roughly equal in size and long, narrow shape, linked beneath a picturesque stone bridge with the kind of arch which, when combined with its reflection, forms a perfect circle. A linear park or greenway looped around one of the ponds and ranked high with the dating crowd for late-night assignations. Such popularity was well-documented in the carvings that coated the huge beech trees along the shores, like "Joe-n-Tina 4-eva." During the day it was pretty sleepy. The other pond had stretches of grass along the banks, bordered by narrow streets with immaculate little Victorian houses on the far side, overlooking the water. The banks appeared almost like extensions of the lawns. A great spot to live, at least until we came along. The pond on the park side would have afforded us the privacy to fish and frolic in any manner we chose, but for some reason held far fewer fish than the homey side. So we would set up camp on the virtual front yards, early, and have at it.

Our quest was that Prince of Mud, the carp. We didn't have any preconceived notions about the carp, it swam and ate and fought and we thought it was the greatest thing we'd ever done to catch a big one. In a couple of years we would have a falling out, ditch the bottom-feeder to make time with a classier babe like a bass or even a trout. Eventually we'd rekindle the affair. I guess you never forget your first carp. At that age, it was the purest form of fun. We'd arrive on single-speed bikes, adorned with spinning rods, snacks, iced tea, tackle boxes, a metal stringer clanging with optimism, and a transistor radio. And, of course, the critical ingredient, a loaf of Wonder bread. A trip to the pond provided excellent training for the busboy jobs that loomed only a few years away. Fortunately, single-speed bikes had foot brakes back then.

There were loads of fish in those murky depths, and the food chain was pretty evident. The grassy banks by the roadside were a favorite spot for tourists and locals alike to feed the mallards and Pekings that called the place home (believe it or not, back then Canada geese were a rare, even thrilling sight). The smaller fish sat tight below the ducks and waited for crumbs. The bigger ones formed schools and patrolled the surface along the shoreline, cruising for spongy crusts that had escaped notice or been ignored by bloated birds. The popularity of this pond over the other wasn't chance after all, it was a case of feast or famine.

Displaying our incipient fishing acumen, we figured out that to catch fish we had to insert ourselves into the food chain. Carp may generally like cheese or corn or worms, but the average tourist didn't feed these things to the ducks. So we began approximating the crumbs with tiny, yeasty Pillsbury doughballs and promptly caught legions of carp, our baseball-sized bobbers burrowing wide wakes to all corners of the pond. But this was the sophomore set, we wanted the seniors. The ones in the gang. A meeting required either patience until they came along or a more proactive, mobile search. So we'd bike along the streets and when a slurping, sloshing school was spied we'd pull over, determine its direction of travel and begin chumming in the eventual path. Then add a couple of hook-infused crusts into the mix. Soon we were hanging with the varsity crowd.

The drawback to this method was that chumming the fish looked a lot like feeding the ducks, to the ducks that is. The whole pondful would come sailing over in wild excitement. This could and did lead to some ugly situations. Turn your back to get a bite of your buttered roll and your line is flying away and *up*. We may have displayed some typical boyhood-sadistic tendencies in those days but we didn't want any part of this noisy, messy scene and neither for that matter did the big carp. They'd scatter and disappear in seconds. We had to ward off the descending flock, *before* the fish arrived. Yelling and waving branches and throwing first pebbles and then stones, we managed to rebuff their advances. At the same time, we unwittingly took on the appearance of two *very* cruel young men. The Victorian homeowners peered through their lace curtains in horror. The ASPCA was contacted. Our carp fishing days were over, for a while.

It was time to graduate to the next level anyway. At nine years old I was clearly sophisticated enough to do battle with the intelligentsia at the exclusive mill pond one town over. The setting was idyllic, with a

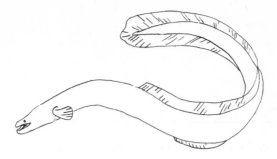

American Eel

former grist mill, water wheel and all, at one end, stately willow trees, the works. There were some native trout but mostly a stocked population, along with bass, sunfish, carp, eels and so on. Fishing here required joining the tony Mill Pond Fishing Club, with its 100-member limit, painful $25 annual fee and God-awful boring monthly meetings. But as the newest and youngest member I won first place in their yearly Opening Day contest once and second place twice, over a four-year span. My technique had sharpened, my bobbers shrank to the size of cherry tomatoes. Then they were gone altogether and I was using a hypodermic needle to inject a little buoyancy into a big nightcrawler. Or threading on a purple Roostertail or a Mepps black fury. I swear that once I even caught a fish on a Daredevil, although there were no witnesses. I was hot stuff.

The Mill Pond was a step up in competition and a move toward the mainstream. But my offbeat nature was not to be denied. The pond had easy access in one section only, and, needless to say I was convinced that the biggest, surliest native trout were hiding elsewhere. So I proceeded to venture through thickets and over bogs, hopping from one skunk cabbage to the next, as I worked my way to the most distant fallen tree in the hope that a giant grandaddy brown was residing in its shadow. In one or two cases this was true, but generally the trout here behaved like the carp at the twin ponds. They too waited for the bloody tourists to arrive with their bags of starch. Even so, the trips to the far reaches of the pond were a lot of fun. The most extreme case of manifest destiny occurred one summer when the gates that controlled the flow for the mill were vandalized. The water level fell dramatically. This exposed the muddy bottom from the back yard of, who else, a mean old lady, all the way out to an island in the middle. Given that I could barely afford to pay the membership fee, a boat was out of the question. To my mind, the island had grown to fabled heights. It was unquestionably the resort of the large and famous. Tossing boards and rocks in front of me as I went, I constructed a build-as-you-go bridge to the promised land. At times I was off-target and up to my thighs in fetid muck, and ended up using the boards as a kind of life preserver to extract myself. To make matters worse, all this mess was for nothing. When I reached my destination what I found was a mixed-use facility providing nesting grounds for swans and snapping turtles and luxury accommodations for water rats and snakes. I hadn't reasoned that any shoreline normally inhabited by fish would be too shallow to sustain life under these depleted circumstances. So much for island paradise. I retreated to the mainland with my tale between my legs.

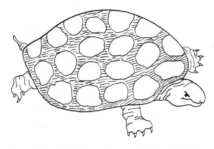

On the subject of snapping turtles, the ones in this pond were positively prehistoric, far beyond anything I've seen since. Mill Pond fisherman lore had it that they kept the duck population in check with periodic *Jaws* imitations. Although I never witnessed such carnage, I had good reason not to doubt it. The accessible pond frontage consisted of a stone retaining wall against several feet of water. Our catch was hung on a stringer and tied off to a root. This kept the fish alive and fresh indefinitely. It also acted on occasion as a homing device for the giant reptiles. Where there had been three trout, now there were two! We were less than pleased about sharing our dinner. The last straw came early one Sunday morning when I reached down to add a nice rainbow to my growing collection. The fish had been flopping around in the dirt so I took him by the gill with one hand, lowered him into the water and began to wipe him off with the other. As my hand moved down his length, it slid directly into the mouth of a monstrous snapper poised to chomp on the tail. The timing was impeccable. He closed right on my hand, slicing my index finger to the bone. I was inches from his head, which was about as big as my own. He must have released momentarily and I sprang back from the edge. It was the only time in my life that I went into a state of shock. I kept staring at my hand, counting the digits and trembling. After a minute or two I snapped out of it and ran wailing to a physician's house that lay just down the street.

"Doc, there's a turtle the size of a Buick over there!"

"Don't worry, son, I don't care how you got this. I'm just going to fix it up for you, okay?"

"But it's true. He could be on his way over here right now to finish the job!"

"Now look here, young man. I've seen you climbing around that mill. I wouldn't be surprised if you were the same little smart-ass that let the water out of the pond. I don't condone your behavior and look where it's gotten you, your finger's pretty mangled. My advice is to behave a little more responsibly from here on out. But this stays between you and me, how does that sound?"

It sounded pretty good. Not only were the turtles attacking, now they were getting me framed. Fact is, no one ever believed us, the big boys only showed themselves very early in the morning when they figured no one was around. But I knew who they were, and vengeance would be mine. A few days later I was back. I gripped a dead sunny in my bandaged hand and inserted a large treble hook with the other. I attached the sunwich to one end of a rope and the ensemble to a thick, live branch on an old maple tree that overhung the pond in the main corner. The branch would act as a round-the-clock turtle rod. I wasn't sure what the next step would be, but this was a good beginning. The next day I returned to find sunfish, hook, rope and the entire branch torn off and missing. I had to concede, I was overmatched. The turtles ruled. In fact, they're probably still there and, extrapolating to present size, may even have taken the village by now.

As spring turned to summer, the trout got predictably lethargic and the catches dwindled. We'd abandon our rods to join the other kids for a few slides down the wooden ramp that directed the overspill, or do cannonballs off the turtle tree (owing to my previous encounter, I positioned myself at the back of the line). For a boy aspiring to the likes of Huck Finn, fishing was just the start of a day at the pond. The grist mill was active only on special occasions when townsfolk would get dressed up like olden times and put on a reenactment of the milling process for tourists. The rest of the year it was locked up. As the doctor alluded to earlier, in fishing downtime we would crawl over, under and around this ancient structure, and eventually we appropriated it as our very own fisherman's fort. By sidestepping across the hub of the waterwheel and slipping between the stone foundation and one of the spokes, we had discovered a narrow passage that led into the mill. The final opening was a squeeze through thick slime, water splashing all around, but once inside all was quiet and dry. From this new hideout we could relax, eat our mid-morning snacks, and peek through the cobwebs at the camera-toting tourists who came to stuff the ducks and gawk at the natural beauty. As they turned to get a shot of a classic grist mill, they may also have gotten a shot in the head from a peashooter poking out through a cracked windowpane. No eyes were put out, but the rumor of a haunted grist mill was born.

The freshwater options in my area were limited, it was primarily a coastal scene with stripers and blues reigning supreme. I did my share of saltwater fishing in those days, but without a boat or a surf-casting rod I stuck mostly to a saltwater creek down the street from my house. It held flounder, blackfish, assorted undesirables and, in July and August, as many snapper blues as you could catch. It was really more of a freshwater experience that happened to be conducted in saltwater. My preferences always leaned that way

and still do. We would hold contests to see who could catch the most baby blues, the winner sometimes reaching triple digits. The Sidewinder and the Skipjack were two little silver lures that looked pretty much like the dozens of other silver lures on the tackle shop shelf, but something about their shapes made them deadly snapper assassins. One time my reel malfunctioned and the lure started dragging the bottom. When I got it going and pulled up, I had managed somehow to hook a toadfish. If you've never seen a toadfish, consider yourself lucky. The toadfish doesn't get too big in size, but it is a bottom-dwelling, shell-crushing son-of-a-bitch that can inflict serious damage if you happen to stroll over one. Wading barefoot in the creek was to be avoided at all costs. The kid at the end of the block was said to have an older brother with a missing toe. I made a point of wearing my Converse Chucks at all times.

As I grew so did my sense of angling adventure and, still traveling on two wheels, expanded my search to a river nearly fifteen miles away. After a few disappointing trips I recognized the need for a craft. There were whole stretches that were beyond even my pioneer spirit and a pair of gardening shears. A good buddy and neighbor of mine, Chris B., had recently purchased a two-person inflatable, so he was rightfully and rapidly promoted to number-one accomplice. On one ill-fated morning we somehow stuffed the entire boat into a full-blown, aluminum rack backpack and headed out. We must have looked ridiculous, but the traffic was light at 4 a.m. Several hours later we arrived at the barbed wire fence that discouraged entrance to the hallowed, fly fishing-only section of the river. Anglers would pay handsomely for a few hours on a specific segment of river. Each run had its limits defined by metal poles with a numeric designation, one to twelve, poking just above the surface of the water in the river's center. Penniless outsiders such as ourselves had no idea about the existence of any of this, much less the strict protocol; we knew only that beyond this fence and through those dense, swampy woods lay hundreds of yards of remote, seldom-fished territory. The raft went over, we slid under. Carving a path to even a single launching site was difficult, but we managed to break through and stood at the banks of our latest conquest. Using a foot pump to blow up the boat, we slid into the surprisingly strong current and were in business. Paddling upstream through the narrow, snaking river, we tied off to trees and bushes as we reached a fishy spot, or simply to rest. The undercut banks concealed large numbers of hungry fish, and we were having a field day. Continuing upstream, rubber creel beginning to swell, we soon arrived at the last of the runs, #12. We had no idea what this cryptic marker represented, and rowed right on by. Then came #11, which we actually tied off onto for some excellent fishing. Then a long stretch before #9. Were these some typically-irrelevant, state-mandated designations?

Only nine fly fishermen were working the river that morning, which had bought us a little more time and a lot more fish. But the picnic was over. We passed the #9 marker and came around a bend right into the float of a very serious dry-fly fisherman. I think in his astonishment he actually dropped his rod. "What the *Hell* are you DOING in here?!" he managed to blurt out as his confusion turned quickly to anger. We were as surprised as he was. For a second I actually thought, "What the Hell are *you* doing here, this is our new favorite spot!" Then it all started to fall into place, the numbers, the fly fishing attire, the many and curiously-hungry fish. We were *way* out of bounds. He was only a few feet away, and he was getting closer. We had to get out of there, immediately.

We started backpaddling into the current and sailed past the #9 marker going full-tilt. The fly fisherman started receding into the distance, gesticulating wildly and yelling something. There was no way he was going to catch us, we were off scot-free. Suddenly we plunged headlong into the missing #10 marker that had lurched over and was now pointing *upstream* a few inches below the surface. The boat deflated instantly as a gaping tear swallowed up gallons of river. "We got away, but now we're going to DIE!" The water was over our heads, the tackle boxes and rods swirled around us as we drifted downstream.

Somehow we got hold of most of our belongings and swam to shore, soaked to the skin and freezing.

We weren't going to do any more fishing just now. In fact, we might not ever come back to this spot, at least for a few weeks. If we could just get back to the bikes, hidden under piles of leaves, and out into the streets, we'd pass for couple of kids on a Saturday trip to the candy store. Yes, and somewhere along the way we had run into a very intense sun shower. We scrambled through the brush, trying to retrace our steps, but this was much further upstream than where we had put in. We came upon some paths. Fly fishermen paths, no doubt. It didn't matter, we had to get out of here as fast as possible, and the  paths offered the least resistance. Just then we saw someone up ahead. We weren't sure they'd seen us. Chris B. must have thought it was a bear, or some equally menacing ground-dweller. He climbed a tree. I stood frozen and started concocting the type of story that gets one out of dicey situations. I had become quite good at it, but this particular situation was a real challenge. Let's see... we're from out of state, that's a given. No, we're from out of the country, we're from France! Wait, I don't speak French. And Chris B. looks like the Dutch Boy Paint kid. Whatever the story, there's the matter of the fish.

We had managed to save a pair of brown trout from the creel but had lost the rest and the creel itself. As the stranger drew nearer I dropped the fish to the ground and in a stroke of genius decided to stand on them. The stranger was upon me.

"Hey, how're ya doin'?"

"Good, how are you?"

"Oh, just fine. Say, did you know this is private property?"

"No sir, I was just fishing downstream and worked my way up."

"Past the dam and the barbed wire fence?"

"I didn't see anything like that. Part of the way up I couldn't get to the river so I had to go back into the woods." I was so slippery.

"I see you got a couple."

Ouch. I stepped off the flatfish. "Yeah, a couple."

"Nice browns. Well, like I say this is private property and you can get a fine of $250 for being in here illegally. So you'd better head out." Still looking straight at me, "And your friend too."

He turned and walked away.

We were crestfallen. This guy hadn't fined us or taken our fish or pummeled us, but he had made us feel small, really small. Our little game was as plain as day to him, that was the shame of it. And he hadn't even had time to get an update from Fly Fisherman #9.

But he helped me, that fellow. He put me on the track which I've followed to this day. The energy of the offbeat angler was still burning inside me, but I needed to channel it in a positive, or at least legal direction. As jobs came along so did money and cars and the ability to get to places that offered sanctioned adventure. Saving up for six months one long winter, I finally had enough to buy my first fly rod. In college I met Sebastian, who had been raised under the tutelage of a fly-fishing Pop from old Ireland. He encouraged me toward the fishing life described elsewhere in *The Offbeat Angler*. Sure, being bad feels pretty good, but you can get that sort of satisfaction in more creative ways *within* the boundaries of propriety. If not for The Man in the Woods, I might have lost my way, appeared on a post office wall, or worse, given up fishing.

And that would have been *very* bad.

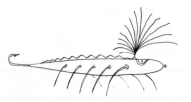

The Low Down Chummin' Blues

By Sebastian O'Kelly

Chris and I are known for our diversions and you might think upon seeing its title that this chapter will lead to a discussion of the Chicago jazz scene. Of course, my fellow afishionado, we also pride ourselves on our fishing puns–the good, the bad, and the ugly. In that case, you should quickly figure out that I am going to talk about chumming for bluefish. Then you will hear about that magical and poetic combination of chumming and fly fishing for blues and stripers. There are other unexpected combinations you will find in this story. Read on.

What, say you, chum and fly fish? Isn't that like wearing sneakers and cut-offs to hear the National Symphony play at the Kennedy Center? Then at the reception afterwards, sprinkling Tabasco sauce on your Beluga caviar, taking care to separate it on your plate from the Skoal dip stored for later re-use, while regaling the Farnesworths about your trip last week to a monster truck exhibition in La Plata?

Chumming and fly fishing are seemingly an oil (menhaden that is) and water combination that will undoubtedly leave traditionalists cold. But offbeat angling is nothing if not about attitude, and the right one here might leave you with a smile on your face and perhaps a trick to try for those blues and stripers when they can't be found and caught otherwise. Chasing breaking fish on the surface crashing bait, with diving birds as your guide, is the way to go on the salty long rod these

days. But it is not an everyday occurrence and sometimes you have to
try something different.

My on-again, off-again romance with the greasy bucket dates to my
pre-fly fishing childhood and my first introduction to fishing in the salt,
courtesy of my dad or "old man" as I referred to him (not always affectionately) later in my teen years. We went out of Montauk, NY on a
party boat one August and left my mom and two younger brothers to
frolic on the beach where we were staying for vacation. I think I was
about nine at the time. I remember getting very little sleep the night
before and firing out of bed as soon as the alarm went off in a way to
this day only happens when a fishing trip is impending. We were to be
targeting fish that were far bigger than anything I had ever pursued in
my freshwater life; in fact, my largest fish to date would have been just
about bait-size for the gorilla blues in the pictures posted on the marina
bulletin board.

The big boat chugged out of the harbor and I sat outside the cabin
watching the two twentyish deckhands getting gear and tackle ready,
their hands moving quickly and surely, their bare arms dark with sun
and rippled with muscle. I thought how cool those guys were and
wished I could be a boat mate one day. In the corner stood a small,
dirty machine with an open maw and outtake pipe. It belched diesel
fumes and rattled and shook like a washing machine with a busted belt.
One of the men fed whole menhaden—known as pogies or bunker in
some parts, kind of like how sub sandwiches are called heros, grinders,
or hoagies depending on where you get them—by the armful into the
maw, using a sawed-off broom handle to stir the fish up or poke the
occasional stubborn one into the grinder. The machine hummed and
vibrated as it worked on the menhaden before spitting a viscous, oily
glop out the outtake into a bucket, the diesel smell now mixed with the
rich, pungent stink of masticated fish. I was alternately fascinated and
repulsed, as only a young kid can be when he sees a machine that can
do such a powerful and brutal thing.

"That's the chum," my dad said. "They ladle it out into the current
and it attracts the fish to the surface. We will be drifting menhaden
back into the slick caused by the chum."

I nodded, not saying a word and completely engrossed.

That day I saw what the wonders of chum could do, producing my
first bluefish, a brute that left my arms sore and a bruise under one
where I fought him with the rod. He won me third place in the party
boat pool. That night in bed, while I watched the room swing softly
back and forth—the aftereffect of the day spent on the rocking boat— I
pressed against the bruise to remind me of that fish, now dissected
and resting in a fridge in my parents' room, that it was real and that I
really did catch it. The trip also produced an unquenchable desire to

return, made all the worse by the fact that we lived miles from the ocean and the trip to the beach was only a once a summer kind of thing. But it was enough to keep the interest running deep and the thought of strong fish straining my biceps during many a slow winter's class.

My next-most vivid chumming memory came a couple of years later when my dad, along with his friend Werner, planned a night party boat trip off the Jersey Shore, land of big hair, big talkers, and, most importantly, big blues (it would be another couple years before I became interested in fishing for those with big hair). I was even more excited than normal. A night trip! Who knew what monster fish loomed in the dark waters beyond the lightline? And for a kid, whose regular, strictly-enforced bedtime was 9 o'clock, to stay up until 2 or 3 in the morning doing what he loved most–how could you beat that?

We set off at dusk and almost immediately Werner went inside "to take a rest." He is a big Bavarian with legs thicker than my waist, a chest broader than a keg at the Hofbrau Haus, and hands the size of hockey gloves (his favorite sport). But his semi-circular canals proved to be more sensitive than a ballerina's and we would only see Werner emerge on deck a couple of times that night. On this trip, my dad was determined not to use the tackle provided by the boat, pool cue rods the diameter of my wrists and winch-strength bait-casting reels spooled with line strong enough to tether a bull moose. My dad was a big believer in light tackle and giving the fish a sporting chance and in that respect he was certainly ahead of his time, particularly as it pertained to party boat tackle protocol. He had rigged up three long and limber surf-casting rods with spinning reels spooled with 15-pound test and hooks used to catch smaller flounder. We had gotten some funny looks

from the mate when we bought our bait but my dad was determined to show everybody the virtue of the sporting way.

It was an entirely male clientele that night, mostly hard hat types who lived and worked in gritty cities like Bayonne in factories that have long since been shuttered and moved offshore to Mexico or Taiwan where labor is cheap. Up in the bow was a cluster of a dozen older men who joked around like they knew this voyage and each other well. I was the youngest on board, but I was used to this from previous trips and took pride in the compliments ("That's a nice fish, kid... Hey, that one is almost as big as you.") from other passengers when boating a good fish.

We chugged to a stop and the Captain sounded the horn, the signal to drop our lines. We fed unweighted chunks of menhaden into the current. They drifted into the blackness and I wondered if there were sharks out there. *Jaws* had just come out and while I was not old enough to be allowed to see it, big sharks were very much on the brain. The mate moved to the stern, dipping a long-handled ladle in a stew of chum in a large grey trash bin–of the kind you see in cafeterias–and flinging it out, several consecutive tosses in a row to get the slick started. Our rods jutted out a good four feet from everyone else's. I could touch the water with my rod tip if I wanted but I knew from lots of lectures from my dad that you were supposed to keep your tip up at all times.

A fisherman just below us hooked a fish, then another guy tied into one. Shortly, our rods were bent with blues that we worked to the boat before the mate gaffed them and hoisted them onto the deck, where they flopped everywhere, mouths regurgitating menhaden. My dad and I pinned them with our knees, the slime warm and greasy against my skin, and dropped them into a burlap bag tied to the rail. My dad sent me into the cabin to get Werner, now prone on a bench, but Werner waved me off with one of his big mitts without even looking up. We nailed a couple more before the action slowed and the Captain moved us to another stop. Werner made a brief appearance to get "a few breaths of fresh air" and then headed back inside, his face as pale as a pompano.

The horn sounded, lines were fed out. The bite was on and my dad and I were hooking up regularly with a bigger grade of blues that were really giving our light tackle a test. If you ever fish on a party boat, particularly a crowded one, line management–and thereby fish management–becomes critical, because a wayward blue with a hook in the lip and a mind of its own (they almost all have one, peanut-sized that it may be) can zig-zag along the boat across all those lines, creating the mother of all bird nests and screwing up the fishing for those entangled for a good fifteen minutes while the mate cuts the lines free. There are two ways to control a rampaging blue. One is to horse the fish as it gets close to the boat so there is no chance to take off on a tangent— not really a feasible option for us with our relatively light line and noodly rods. The other is to pursue more of a Woodward and Bernstein approach, except that you are following the fish instead of the money. So if you are in the stern and the fish heads for the bow, you follow it on up. This requires that you slide under the rods and lines of those in your path, an inconvenience to them but one most gladly accommodated because they'll likely need the favor returned once they have a fish on. Of course, if you are the ones hooking most of the fish and they're not...

Which was what was happening with the old-timers in the bow. I'm not sure why we were out-fishing them. Maybe it was the lighter line that allowed our baits to sink deeper than theirs. Or maybe our stern position allowed us a further drift from the boat. Or maybe it was the Fish God blessing us at that moment in time. But after our second or third run up there with bow-streaking blues, an older gentleman with a salt and pepper beard pointedly told my father that if we used heavier tackle, we wouldn't need to invade their space. My father said something about light tackle being a much better and more sporting way to fish, at which point the gentleman turned and said, "We is heah for da fish, not for da fishin'."

My father, never one to back down when challenged, pointed to the big blue thrashing on the surface at the end of his line, and in what could best be described as a bad cross between Irish brogue and 1970s street jive replied, "We is heah for da fish and for the da fishin'!" Good thing the mate was there, gaff in hand, before any trouble could start.

This was a story that my father polished, embellished with a light Irish touch, and retold many times over the years to mostly receptive audiences. It was quickly entered into The Patrick O'Kelly Hall of Fame for Tales along with such favorites as how he "bedded" two Miss Irelands when he was young, and the day he spent giving Walt Disney a tour of Dublin after a chance meeting in a bar the night before. Those stories bring a smile now when I think of them, though there were more than a few that I was less than enamored of (his retelling of my first track race, which I ran in a favored pair of heavy workboots and came in close to last, being my least favorite). Whatever my old man's pluses and minuses, stories, myths, and half-truths, I did have him to thank for those early fishing experiences that have led to my current obsession.

After that trip, my piscine pursuits took a turn inland and focused on the freshwater side for the next twenty years. I acquired a real job, house in the 'burbs, and a very pregnant wife (though Liz would not approve of the verb in this sentence). But timing, circumstance, and, most importantly, a friend with a boat conspired to encourage me to give the salt another try. The Chesapeake Bay, a hotspot for blues and stripers, was only an hour away. I had been reading about the whole saltwater fly fishing phenomenon and had bought an eight-weight earlier in the year and was eager to give it a try.

I gave Liz a kiss that October morning. She was due with our first in a week, but felt fine and had convinced herself that the doctor had gotten it wrong and the baby was two weeks away. My wife is nothing if not precise and wasn't going to settle for some HMO doc's estimate if she felt otherwise. So I felt comfortable heading out, but we agreed to stay in touch during the day.

J.P. and I met off Route 50 at Angler's, a way station for Bay-area hunters and fishermen. It was our second trip that fall. J.P. is an ex-Marine aviator, prompt and organized. He is very welcome for it as I've reached the age where one is less than willing to tolerate goofing around and delay in advance of a trip. We stocked up on a few Clousers and a couple of jigs.

"What about getting some chum?" I asked when we got to the counter. "You mentioned a spot where there's a lot of chumming." On our previous trip, we had been chum-less.

"I thought we were fly fishing."

"We are. But we may want to mix things up." I could see that he was not entirely comfortable with the proposition. His girlfriend Holly told me that J.P. was absolutely fastidious about his boat—an open-deck 22-footer designed more for cruising than fishing—and spent more time prepping and cleaning it than riding in it. His body language was not hopeful.

But like any Marine, J.P. prided himself on his problem-solving skills. I saw the wheels turning behind those cool Ray Bans. Then he answered. "We can hang it over the side in a bag."

Problem solved, we made the purchase. We drove to the Naval Academy where J.P.'s ex-mil status gets boating privileges that a civvie like I will never have. After a goodly amount of time unrolling the boat's tarp and loading the boat up, with everything put in J.P.'s assigned places—he was particularly careful handling the still-frozen chum—we hit the water. The sun was already up, presaging a warm Indian summer day. He put the boat up on a plane as we sped from the mouth of the Severn River out into the Bay. J.P.—his eyes scanning the horizon, face expressionless, thick hair ruffling in the wind, windbreaker flapping to the side, the sunglasses perched perfectly on a straight nose—could have doubled as a model in a J. Crew catalog. He was as comfortable steering the boat as he was swooping through the air in an A-6. We zoomed around for the next couple of hours searching for diving birds and breaking fish, to little avail, before heading down to the Hill.

Located near the entrance to Eastern Bay, the Hill is a large underwater hump that causes an upwelling in the Bay's currents, concentrating plankton and baitfish, and—by extension—predators such as blues and stripers. It's well-known and a favored spot of the chumming brigade. At peak times, boats fish literally bumper to bumper and gallons upon gallons of ground menhaden are dumped into the water in order to spur the bite. One well-known Bay fly fishing guide has been trying to get chumming banned as he thinks it causes disease in the striper population. His views are persona non grata on the Hill, a lazy man's kind of place where you can anchor up, flip on the radio, sling some chum, float some cut bait, and take in the view.

The view is anything but scenic, flat water looking over to a line of low marshland. But what makes it interesting are the characters and boats that come to fish here. You see all manner of shapes and sizes (people and boats both)—14-foot camouflage john boats that must give the Coasties safety people heebie-jeebies; 20-25-foot middle class cruisers like J.P.'s; $200,000 plus Chris Crafts with tinted windows; old crab boats retrofitted to carry fishing charters; and, of course, those big party boats, most of whom berth at Deale or Chesapeake Beach on the western shore of Maryland. As for people, there's everyone from the rich, lawyer-lobbyists, to the hard hats from Dundalk ('Dundawk') in Baltimore ('Bawlmore'), to snow-birds who summer in Annapolis.

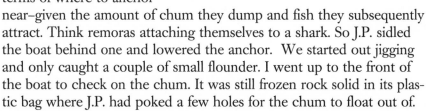

The party boats are where it's at—at least in terms of where to anchor near—given the amount of chum they dump and fish they subsequently attract. Think remoras attaching themselves to a shark. So J.P. sidled the boat behind one and lowered the anchor. We started out jigging and only caught a couple of small flounder. I went up to the front of the boat to check on the chum. It was still frozen rock solid in its plastic bag where J.P. had poked a few holes for the chum to float out of.

"It ain't happening," I said.

"Jab with this," J.P. answered, handing me a knife. "Then dip it up and down in the water."

I leaned over the rail and started picking away but soon figured out that Antarctica would thaw faster. "This isn't working. Where's your bucket?"

J.P. frowned at the thought of the chum, inside a bucket or not, inside his immaculate craft.

I pressed him. "C'mon, we won't get it to work otherwise."

He kept his cool but gave in. "Under the front seat. Just be careful that you don't splatter any on the carpet."

I got to work attacking the chum in the bucket with the knife after I filled it partway with water. The water soon turned a muddy chocolate color. Flecks of chum and fish scales stuck to the sweat on my fore-arms. It was in the seventies now and the sun was hot on my neck and I wondered about getting a sunburn, usually not your typical worry on a late October day. After awhile, I'd hacked away half the block. We had enough to get started after J.P. located a spoon.

I threw out a few spoonfuls like an Army cook slinging the hash at mess time. The tide had fully shifted and the current was moving, a good sign. I pulled out my fly rod and cast in the direction of the slowly sinking chum. I fed out a few more feet of line and gave the Clouser some time to sink before stripping back. After a few strips, the line tightened–fish on! I soon landed a small schoolie striper. J.P. joined me in the fray and over the next hour, between alternating turns at the chum bucket, we consistently caught small stripers and blues before the action slowed.

We are interrupted by the throb of a heavy engine and the wash of another boat. A cigarette boat wannabe schusses past us and swirls back in a "U," sending a heavy bow wave across us before idling to a stop. There are two men and women on board, the latter scantily-

enough clad for me to discretely reach for J.P.'s binoculars. The bikini-clad babes look like the type that would raise their shirts at Mardi Gras for a few beads or put their names on a waiting list to get on the Howard Stern Show. They have a hard look to their heavily made-up faces, with hair permed and teased. The brunette has a large butterfly tattoo at the base of her back. I look for other tattoos and piercings but don't see any before I focus on other salient features for a minute. The guys look pretty cheesy. One of them looks to be using a mousse product even oilier than our chum, its sheen reflecting in the sun.

I see J.P. peering over intently and offer him the binocs. He shakes his head. I forget that the man has 20-15 vision. One of the guys flips on a radio and booming over the water we hear Guns N Roses's "Welcome to the Jungle." There's nothing quite like false casting to the raspy voice of Axl Rose. One of the couples starts to dance, while the other guy searches the coolers for some frosty ones. There are two rods, appropriately standing straight up and stiff, in rod holders at the back of the of the boat but it's is clear that the only angling that will take place today will happen on board.

I lower the binocs and think of my promise to Liz. "Where's your cell phone?" I ask. J.P. points to a backpack up in the bow. I try dialing but get no tone. I flip it to J.P. "It's not working."

He looks it over. "Battery's dead." I don't linger on it and we resume fishing. The bite picks up and we are back into fish, our attention only interrupted briefly when the cigarette boat zooms away, presumably to find a more intimate place on the Bay. Soon, the chum is finished and we are too, sunburned and fished out. We ride back to Annapolis and my thoughts turn again to Liz.

It's been a good pregnancy and we've tried to enjoy the freedom of the last several months–at the same time planning and preparing for the new arrival–recognizing we are in for big changes. We have taken the proverbial shopping runs to find a good crib; thumbed through the catalogs for the safest swings; read all the hot books on baby rearing; consulted with other new parents on sleep strategies; attended the ritual birthing classes; and resolved that I would be standing near her head, not her feet, when the magic moment arrived. It was all a little over the top, but what do you expect from first-time parents. Still, we made time for some fun and travel. Last weekend was spent lolling around at a bed and breakfast at St. Michaels on the Eastern shore.

J.P. and I soap and scrub every last square inch of the boat, per J.P.'s rules. I'm antsy to get home and think J.P.'s fastidiousness–"Seb, remember to scrub underneath by the prop"–is too much but as his guest I don't feel I'm in a position to complain. We finally finish and I split.

I arrive home to a quiet and dark house. I wonder where Liz is, conclude she is probably out for a walk–she has been walking a lot during the pregnancy to stay fit–and throw some bacon on the pan for a sandwich. I walk upstairs to check the phone messages. No red light is blinking. I call our friends and neighbors Ted and Andrea to see if she is up there.

Liz had just called them after being unable to reach me–she is in the hospital! I scramble to finish my sandwich–a man needs fuel as much as a woman does for this sort of marathon–grab a toothbrush and a sweatshirt and fly out of the house. The hospital is only a mile away and I reach the maternity ward in no time. My wife is walking around with early contractions, looking no worse for wear, and not knowing whether to hit or hug me.

Six hours later a healthy 7 pound 3 ounce keeper named Sheridan is born.

I've been fishing on the Bay more than a few times since. When she's old enough, I've resolved to take Sheridan (and now her brother Dermot) with me and explain to her the circumstances surrounding her birth. I'll even demonstrate to her the art of chumming and wonder if she'll have the same fascination for it that I did as a kid. I hope she'll take to it, or at least to fishing, and one day fly fishing.

However, I realize the chum/ fly fish option may not be for everyone. It's not something you'll see featured in the latest Trout Unlimited calendar. Others may find the ethics of it troubling, not to mention cleaning the menhaden residue off their lines. However, its effectiveness cannot be looked down upon. And it's really not like wearing cut-offs and sneaks to the Kennedy Center.

But if you give it a shot, I advise you to pick a day when your wife is not giving birth.

Downtown Mr. Brown

By Sebastian O'Kelly

If I were to tell you about catching browns in the city, you would soon be scrambling into the basement to find appropriate fishing gear and a map with all the proper markings for public transit stops. You might also reach for the mace, because in a big city personal safety is always an issue and a fly rod weighing a couple of ounces is just not going to keep a brawny mugger at bay. But any trepidation over safety will be quickly overcome by the exciting thought of catching brown trout where you don't have to bivouac through narrow country roads for three hours to travel 50 miles, or hop on a plane to take you halfway across the country to a popular Rocky Mountain river crowded with half of all the other East Coast fly fishermen.

Yes, I am referring to a brown fish capable of growing to large sizes, a dogged fighter, wary and selective, and prized as a game fish among Europeans in countries from which they originally came from. But after tossing midges in the clear spring creeks in Pennsylvania, staking out a beat on the Test, or waiting your turn on the Beaverkill, you already know all those things and more about browns. You just want to know where you can find them in the big city.

Sadly, you can't. Or least not that I'd ever heard, though maybe you could bore a hole in one of those reservoir pipes that pumps in water from the country and have a chance at snagging one that inadvertently was sucked in the intake from its high mountain, clear sky home. Sorry to disappoint.

But you can catch a brown fish in the concrete jungle that has many of the same characteristics of his more glamorous relation and puts up an even tougher battle on light tackle. I'm talking about the carp. That's right, the lowly, oft-maligned and under-appreciated carp. A brown water fish if there ever was one.

Now before you launch this book at the bin by the refrigerator with a snide remark like, "trash book about a trash fish," bear with me, revise your expectations and read the following story. I think you'll find the carp a worthy quarry on fly tackle–that you don't have to travel far to find.

The Chesapeake and Ohio Canal stretches from Georgetown in the middle of downtown Washington, DC almost 200 miles to Cumberland, Maryland, winding its way through rugged terrain along the banks of the Potomac River. Designed in the early to mid-18th century as an overland waterway to reach the Ohio River (it ends about halfway there) to transport barge cargo pushed by mule, the C & O Canal was considered something of engineering marvel at the time, pushing water a couple of hundred yards uphill through a series of interconnecting locks. Built on the backs of immigrant labor, with help from the occasional stick of dynamite to clear stubborn rock and some giant oaks, at the time it was a public works project that would rival today's space program in ambitious design and brilliant engineering.

The C & O Canal's commercial potential was never fully realized; however, as it was rendered obsolete by the late 1800's by the economically more efficient Iron Horse and Rail. Yet its rustic beauty, pebbled tow-path, and abundant wildlife remained and Congress designated it a National Park in 1971. Since then, millions of tourists and residents alike have hiked and biked its paths, canoed its waters, camped along its shores, studied its history, and found solace in its wildness. Sunfish, channel catfish, carp and the occasional smallmouth or largemouth bass are found in its waters. As you approach near its end in Georgetown, Washington's party scene central, signs start to show that you are entering an urban area–the occasional beer can might be seen floating along the bank; the number of cigarette butts per square yard of path increases; a torn condom wrapper might lie at the edge of the water, detritus from a quickie on the bank from last Saturday night; and the water narrows and darkens in color. Down here, the odd dead body has been found face down in the water, the result of a drug deal gone bad. Dead floaters aside, the canal's environs are cleaner than most urban parks. Most Washingtonians take pride in it and care for it accordingly.

Several years ago, a fellow Trout Unlimited member from our Potomac-Patuxent Chapter told me that in the spring big carp move under the mulberry trees along the canal to feed on the fallen berries. At the time, I filed his comment under the file, "Potentially Useful Fishing Information Tidbits" (PUFIT–you have to expect an acronym from a guy who used to work for the government) and stuffed it into a back drawer of my mind where it remained through the floods of 1996, which blew out the lower part of the canal and most of the fish with it. There the file stayed until this past summer when I had heard that the fish were back–my friend Terry Shultz told me he had spotted sizable swirls in the water while jogging along the towpath. The good fortune of the fish was no doubt enhanced by a generous Congressional appropriation and thousands of volunteer hours that restored the washed out portions of the canal. I also now had a job within striking distance of Georgetown, close enough that I could get over there on a slow day for an hour of fishing and no one would miss me at the office (with two small children, weekend fishing trips must be planned sparingly, carefully and with spousal sensitivity).

Most relevantly, my motivation and ability to try this kind of fishing was probably greater now than ever, even though I had much less time to do it. I still kick myself over the period between my late teens and late twenties when I had all kinds of time to fish but didn't partake of many of the opportunities. Perhaps, it had to do with spending too many Saturdays flat on my back nursing a hangover. Or maybe it was due to a conservative, even pessimistic, view of my fishing skills that when I did venture out I tended toward the tried and true, hitting the "old faithfuls"–spots where I knew the quarry and was assured of reasonable success. There was some experimentation to be sure, and more than a few offbeat experiences, but I certainly didn't take many fishing risks. Now, I was on a mission to recapture my misspent fishing young adulthood, determined to fish more and better in the face of a busy life and the other conundrums of middle age. Call it pushing the fishing edge, while being careful not to lapse into absurdity or extremism, though some might certainly label trying your luck in Georgetown as both.

While mowing the lawn under a big mulberry tree in my backyard early this summer, my TU pal's info uploaded itself from the back drawer into my frontal lobe, perhaps spurred on by the thought of all that yard work. I found a ladder and climbed up looking for fresh specimens on the higher branches. The berry bloom was winding down but I soon found a couple of bigger ones.

My wife Liz came outside. "Are you figuring out how to cut that tree down?" she asked sweetly. She has been nagging me for a couple

of years to be rid of this tree and its carpet-staining berries which our
children inevitably track indoors.

"Um...no."

"Then what are you doing?"

I know better than to be evasive with Liz when she is pursuing a
direct line of questioning. "I'm trying to figure out how to tie a 'mulberry fly'," I mumbled.

"I should have figured." She laughed. She was in a good mood and
for the most part indulges my fishing obsession.

That night I sat down at my vise and pondered how to tie a "mulberry fly," with the real thing as the model. You couldn't exactly turn
to the latest Orvis catalogue for reference. I also didn't know much
about fishing for carp, with the fly or otherwise. I had caught a couple
on corn as a kid and then accidentally once with a woolly bugger while
fishing for bass. On other occasions, I had made half-hearted efforts to
catch them, to no avail, usually while targeting other species. But I
knew enough to know that they were hard to fool.

Yarn seemed to offer the best choice in terms of size and shape for
a mulberry imitation, but it didn't have quite the right texture, nor did I
have any dark purple on hand. Then, in the drawer where I keep all
my hazmat fly tying chemicals, I spied some epoxy and the Edisonian
light of inspiration flickered on.

I lightly tied a berry to a size 8 hook, then covered it with epoxy
and set it to dry. Voila–the "mulberry fly!" It looked quite realistic (after

all it was the real thing!) and the epoxy
gave it a clear finish and a hardness
that would make it castable, something
that would have been impossible with
just the soft berry on the hook. I tied a
couple more, grinning at the thought
of the repugnant looks from the fly
fishing purists who disdain the use of
any fly not made from natural fur or
feather. Who cares, I thought. These
folks wouldn't be caught dead fishing
for carp in the first place. Members of
the Fly Fishing Order of the Coif could spend endless hours debating
whether my creation might actually qualify as a "fly." Meanwhile, I
would go fishing.

I planned my venture for the Wednesday right before July 4th, when
I knew I had time enough for a long lunch. I cabbed it over to
Wisconsin and M Street and hoofed it down to the canal, its quietness a
nice relief from the bustle of Georgetown. A few folks were walking

down the tow-path, heads down in a hurry to get back to their offices or out of the stifling heat, for your intrepid author and carp fly fisherman wannabe had happened to pick one of the hottest days of the year to try his luck. The weather shaman had issued a Code Red advisory urging folks to stay indoors to avoid the heat and unhealthy levels of ozone in the air—asthmatics and the elderly pay special heed. But dire prognostications issued from inside a heavily air-conditioned building would not be enough to keep this fisherman from trying out his new invention.

I walked a block east until I found a shady tree by a restaurant to eat my lunch. No one was sitting outside on the restaurant veranda— no doubt heeding the Code Red—and while on one level I was glad not to have a crowd watching over my shoulder, not to mention some snooty maitre d' coming over to try to tell me that I couldn't fish there, on another level the fish boaster in me, the one that has me e-mail pictures of my recent fishing expeditions to all my friends, would have liked an audience to play to. As it happened, I was sitting under a large mulberry tree. To my disappointment, there were no berries in the tree. Could I have missed this year's hatch?

I watched the water while I ate and saw lots of small sunfish finning themselves and eagerly slashing at the small doughballs I made from my sandwich and tossed in. All the surface activity by the sunnies triggered a response by something bigger, actually a couple of "somethings" bigger, as two carp of about 10 pounds each surfaced like a pair of German U-boats. I wolfed down the remainder of my sammy and quickly strung up my rod. Mindful of the limited space in back of me, I spotted the carp again and cast.

The first fish moved toward the 'mulberry fly' but swirled off at the last second and disappeared, the other big one actually nudged it but missed inhaling it into his mouth. I cast again but my presentation was sloppy and I put the fish down. I waited for awhile, but those carp were now as scarce as a couple of right-wingers at a Hillary Clinton fundraiser. I made a few more casts and drifted my fly in the current, allowing it to sink and—lo and behold—got a tap and set the hook. It was solid, definitely not one of the sunfish, but it didn't take off on a drag ripping run as you would expect from a powerful carp. An older woman in a loose, flowing black dress stopped along the path to watch me play the fish.

"You have a fish!" she exclaimed in a slight accent. "I walk by here every day and never thought any fish are here."

"Sometimes fish are found in obvious places that are actually not so obvious," I answered, trying to sound like a Wise Old Fishing Master.

"Good for you. My husband used to fish canals like this in France.

But fish in here!" She watched me as I landed the fish, a spunky channel catfish, awkwardly sliding it up the bank. "That's a nice one."

"Thank you." I worked the fly free. I slid the catfish back into the water.

"You are not going to eat it?" She smiled brightly.

"I practice catch and release. Most of the time. Plus, they say not to eat fish caught around here."

She shrugged and with a twirl was off down the path. She had a bounce to her step–*joie de vivre* as they say in her home country. Most of the folks who had gone by walked heavily with their heads down, brushing past as if I wasn't even there, their minds occupied and bodies loathing the heat. The woman's friendliness was gratifying compared to the big city indifference shown by the others, a couple of whom I thought would have stopped out of interest. How many guys do see you fishing in Georgetown on any given day? Then I realized what I might find interesting, others might find strange and if there is one thing you learn living and working in a city, it is to stay away from strange people.

I dusted the dry dirt from my shirt and khakis, wiped the fish goo off my hands onto the grass, and moved up the canal where I had some room to stretch a few casts. I was out in the full sun now and I could feel a thin trickle of sweat run down the channel of my back. Only the committed few would fish on a day like this.

Across the canal, a long, newly-windowed brick wall rose up almost flush to the bank. It looked like one of those old warehouses converted to office space, maybe housing a hot PR firm or bustling dotcom or some other up and coming business that likes to be seen as hip and different. I could see a young woman at her desk in a second-story window looking down at me. She looked a year or two out of college, with hair pinned back and a pair of stylish glasses perched on her nose. Her looked lingered while she picked up the phone and I thought I could see a smile on her face.

There was a time–a lot of hair, more than a few pounds and 15 years ago–when I got my share of second looks from women like the one in the window. It was a time when I did more of my fishing in bars than on the water, a time before the comfortable blanket of middle-ageddom and its attendant responsibilities had settled upon me, and my hairline had gone north, east, west and south in a rapid and irreversible fashion.

In an effort to combat my recessive gene, I learned that the follicular snake oil peddled by the pharmaceutical giants made little difference, though the greasy stuff stashed in the back of our bathroom closet could still make a nice dubbing wax if my wife doesn't toss it first. As for the option of first resort for balding men, Liz dissuaded my efforts a few years ago to slide the part down the side of my head in the direction of Comb-overville. In my job then as a Congressional staffer, I used to sit in hearings behind my hirsute future, a Senator whose part began somewhere below the left earlobe, a shank of hair clinging to the film of his scalp which could not be lifted even by the blast of hot air loosed in a full Senate debate. Liz convinced me of the ridiculousness of it ("Think of those wet strands hanging to your shoulder when you get out of the shower.") and of the potential of the more aerodynamic, nearly-shaved look ("You have such a nicely-shaped head... It makes you look intimidating!"), which I still sport to this day.

As for the weight, the additional pounds were offset somewhat by much of it being muscle from pounding heavy metal at the gym. I wasn't your stylish Corvette. But I also wasn't your grandfather's lumbering Oldsmobile. More like your mid-size Camry.

My attention turned back to the young woman. She was talking into the phone. I imagined her best friend on the other end and the conversation going something like this:

Young woman: Hey, it's me. You're not going to believe this, but there is this guy fishing in the canal right outside my office.

Friend: Are you serious? In the canal? That's gross.

Young woman: Yeah. He's waving this long, skinny pole in the air. And it's like a hundred degrees out. It's really bizarre.

Friend: He's probably fly fishing. My dad does it. A lot of older guys are into it.

Young woman (peering closer to the window): I don't think he's that old. He's pretty bald though.

Friend (giggling): I wonder if he put sunblock on his head.

On that less than flattering thought, I walked upstream and out of her line of view. I self-consciously rubbed my scalp. Sunburn was a real issue with my fair Irish skin and I had forgotten to pack my sunscreen in my work bag—how could I have neglected to include it with my notepad, cell phone and Blackberry this morning! I scanned the water, hoping to pick up any movement in its soupy color. Two rock-like shapes emerged on the featureless bottom, but their stillness indicated nothing of interest. I walked a little further toward a footbridge crossing the canal. I noticed scuff marks on my shoes and the strap on my work carry bag was starting to dig into my shoulder. I was losing focus. I doubled back. Maybe the big boys by the restaurant would have settled down by now.

I stopped to look at those two rocks again. Something trailed in the current behind them—some weeds perhaps. Then I saw a flash of yellow and the shape of a goldfish-like tail. Carp!

I readied to cast, taking a little more time to think through my approach. Better to try to float the fly in than shoot a cast straight at them – a mistake I made earlier in dropping the fly right on top of the fish. So I cast upcurrent and let it drift toward them, mending the line and raising the rod tip slightly when it looked like the fly had drifted too deep.

The smaller of the carp peeled off to the side like a car changing lanes. The carp opened its mouth, orange-yellow lips parting. I stripped the line hard and pulled up on the rod. The piscine pug ripped line in a rapid burst and moved into the middle of the canal, first turning downstream and taking line nearly almost to the backing, then in a change of heart running back. The runs were strong more than fast and I worked him back to the bank before he chugged back into the middle and set up station again, using the weight of his body to dig against the force of the rod. He (I'm no fish biologist but in a break of fishing literary tradition I will identify this fish as 'he') pulled this routine two more times before fully tiring.

The bank was steeper here and no net had been packed with the notepad, cell phone or Blackberry. And 2X tippet was not going to be up to the task of hauling up a fish that I estimated was a couple of pounds shy of double digits. So I cranked the leader in past the first couple of guides while dropping down onto my belly and holding the line in a free hand. The fish did me the favor of sliding up on top of a submerged tussock of grass. I reached in with both hands cupped under the belly and raised him up, the fly falling out of its own accord.

The fish was more colorful than I would have guessed, its dark, bark-colored scales lightening to a vibrant golden hue as they reached the belly. The lips were nearly cutthroat orange in color. He was as thick and wide as he was long and I marveled at what a battle it would be to catch one of his bigger friends. I took my time reviving him in the bathtub-warm water. He slowly swam off.

I wiped the sweat from my brow. This shirt would definitely need a change back at the office. I broke down my equipment and caught a cab at M street, reveling in that feeling of a fishing outing well done for a fish that is not easy to fool. There really was nothing quite like that feeling and it was very much worth the discomfort of the heat, dirt, and an imagined conversation that played on my insecurities. I may not get those second looks any more, but I comfort myself with the thought that back in those days I wouldn't have had the motivation or gumption to try this kind of fishing.

Chalk one up for carp, middle-age and the right fishing attitude.

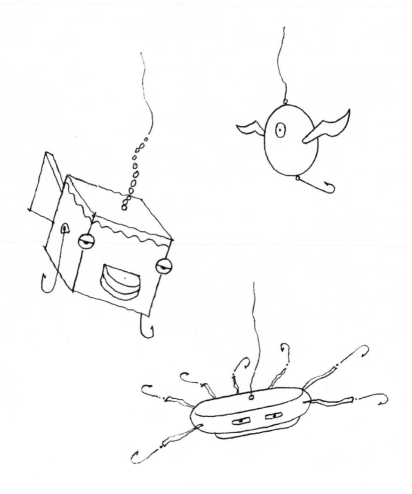

The Sea of Misfit Lures

Quarry Bass

By Christopher Arelt

The working title for this piece was "Rock Bass" which, it so happens, is the common name of a freshwater fish. Readers familiar with the bait-and-hook-swallowing-and-semi-digesting-before-you-know-what's-happened scoundrel can all agree that such a reference, however unintentional, would in all likelihood discourage further reading and possibly induce nausea or, worse, rage. For a tale that actually stars fish as base as the rock bass strays beyond offbeat and into the lunatic fringe. Better to leave them to cavort in the angler's trash bin (being on occasion, in my experience, the nearest patch of dry land) with the other creatures of the day; the sucker, the bagall, the sea robin and the Hell-sent pumpkinseed.

Thankfully, our adventure features not rock but largemouth bass, the kind of bass that don't resort to such covert tactics to get a bite to eat. The Pleistocene parallels lie instead in the location, a rock quarry. Abandoned quarries fill with water to create some of the world's largest built-in swimming pools, and soon become a hotspot for interpretive diving, skinny-dipping and general teenage mayhem. This quarry is somewhat different. For one thing, it's not a rock-walled void but a fairly conventional, sloping depression with a sandy shoreline. For another, the property, though not the quarry itself, is an earthworks operation. Our story is thus set in the shadows of mountains of gravel and sand and amongst massive yellow bulldozers and caterpillars, a kind of parallel universe to the sylvan wonderland of Thoreau.

My initial discovery came by way of referral. A friend and some-time angler stumbled upon it after making a wrong turn while on a jogging expedition nearby. He tested it out in light fashion, found a few fish, mentioned it in passing and apparently lost interest or forgot about it. In my book, this qualifies as a five-star referral. It's close by yet isolated, it's got untold treasures, and nobody, not even the person who told me about it in the first place, fishes there. Obviously, I like competing against fish, not fishermen.

Approaching the quarry is fairly simple in that vehicles many times the size of mine venture in and out daily. Herein also lies the challenge, since the activity limits access from the perspectives of both trespassing and life-safety. At this point I should offer my view on property rights as they pertain to angling. Basically, fishing is next to Godliness and as long as I can get in a backcast there's no reason I can't fish. I don't litter, I throw everything back, I wear a shirt and shoes, sometimes.

It's evening, the quarry is deserted, the yellow monsters are sleeping. As I pull in, I see a new development. My favorite spot, an inlet along the south end, is no more! This has to be a first, the wetlands commission would flip their wigs.

One of the mountains of sand now resides in the inlet, turning it from a viable ecosystem into a barren wasteland with a lone Coke can as the only evidence of organic life. I'm a little discouraged, there were some nice fish living there. But I'm sure they got a sense of what was coming and fishtailed it out. I think of the times I've approached a bank on my stomach to avoid detection. Yes, I'm certain they escaped in time. One opportunity lost is another gained, for a fisherman has to remain optimistic just as a shark needs to swim forward. I've been given real incentive to venture to some of the other areas of shoreline.

There's a lot of earth-moving going on, but the shoreline is not without vegetation. In fact, when I first discovered the quarry there were some pretty sizeable trees. But quarrymen apparently don't care much for trees and some kind of Paul Bunyan-sized hedge clipper

sheared the whole thing to scrub height. This actually made access easier, but not easy, until a recent drought created a bare bank. With care,
virtually the entire perimeter is now fishable. I choose a peninsula on
the far side, formerly inaccessible, as my new favorite spot. If I were a
bass and my home was lost in a case of eminent domain, I'd head for
the peninsula.

About five minutes later I've circumnavigated my way around.
Facing west into the setting
sun I get a sense of how
placid the water is, not the
least bit of a breeze. This is a
good thing. The air temperature is about 70 degrees. Also
a good thing. The bank
slopes gently a rod's length
into the water and then drops
precipitously to an estimated
maximum depth of around 20 feet. The sloping shores are the key to
creating a suitable home for my fine-finned friends. Despite the sand
and rubble, weeds have taken hold in many spots. The scalped brush
hangs over the edge (except in these times of drought), there even
appears to be some regular run-off coming in at one end to inject a little
freshness. The sheer-walled quarries sometimes have fish, but they tend
to be stunted and maybe even have a tentacle or two, although this latter observation may have been my imagination when fueled by some
bronze elixir during days of teenage mayhem.

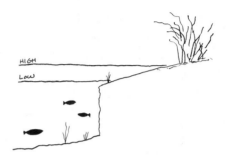

The sun remains high enough for shafts of light to penetrate the
water near shore. I can see a few small bass, about 10 inches, making
their way along the edge of the drop-off. Many are this size. For a time,
I suspected that all the fish in here grew to 10 inches, they were stunted,
and I'd be deja-vuing my way through evenings of instant replay.
Happily, I was mistaken. Up until the evening in question, I had landed
some decent fish with long stretches of routine catches in between.
Tonight would be different.

When I use the term decent fish, it should be qualified that we are
talking about the New England area. As opposed to a romp in central
Florida resulting in a photo with the beet-red face of a grinning angler
straining under the hoisted weight of something that may have been a
bass once, but now looks like an inflatable pool toy or a candidate for
Jenny Craig. New England bass can get big, bigger than you might think,
but they'll never catch up with their Dixie counterparts. Still, they are
long and powerful and, although I can't verify this, I might venture that
similar to humans they're more agile without a soccer ball for a belly.

Time is of the essence when fishing in the evening. In a morning affair there's a chance for success (with admittedly diminishing returns) into the heat of the day, especially if it's overcast. Evening is a race, so it's time to fish or cut bait. I tie on a black popper and toss it sideways along the bank. Instantly, a member of the 10-inch herd latches on. I know without a formal greeting who's come calling, which is okay since it's my first fish. Normally I'm from the bigger-is-better school of thought, but there will forever remain the debate: would you rather catch six 12-inch fish or one 18-inch fish in a one-hour period? What about a two-hour period, or all day? Quantity versus quality, across time. I have created a graph for the reader's comparison with their own standards.

I carefully disengage and release the fish, a good fighter with a chance to grow into a serious contender. Although trash fish are sternly disciplined, real bass get the royal treatment. This system is

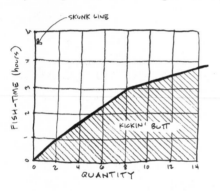

prejudicial and openly unfair, but that's how it goes. You're on my hook now. Casting the same way, I connect with a few more of the increasingly-panicked school as it makes its way along the bank. No sense in passing on a few sure bets to get off the snide. A scattered spray of fruitless casts follows, and I get a sense the peninsula isn't the prime real estate I had appraised. Parking in one spot isn't a case of patience as much as laziness, and I'm a pretty aggressive angler.

Technically, the quarry has two separate bodies of water, I refer to them as upper and lower. The upper one is smaller and governed by a lone private residence, a "McMansion" to use the popular pejorative that sums up the oversized and underconstructed style which is rapid-ly filling up every square inch of marginally buildable land in the Northeast. Word has it that this particular McMansion is home to some surly folks who believe that their proximity to the quarry and its waters is tantamount to ownership. They are reputedly willing and eager to validate this claim, however bogus, with the local authorities.

I'm not looking to get involved in a real estate dispute, at least not without a few burly quarrymen to back me up, but the magnet pull of the unexplored upper quarry is overwhelming. So I cross the 40-foot strip of land that separates upper and lower, rod broken in two as may be required to conceal my intentions, and disappear into a thicket near

the southwest corner of the forbidden quarry.

The water is similar, but the quarrymen's hedgeclippers have not laid waste for some time. As a result there's more structure and shade and greater chance for food along the banks, but casting will be next to impossible. The required improvisation will border on the comical; fortunately, the only onlookers are a pair of noisy crows in a nearby birch. As long as I can deliver the goods to the recipient, my ego is secure. From a crouched position on the bank under the thicket, I might easily lose my balance, stumble a few feet into the water and over the drop-off. This would bring a soggy end to my outing, so I've got to be nimble with my technique. Like a hunchback conducting a bizarre symphony, I manage to contort and flail my way to a pathetic 15-foot extension to my left. The crows intone their discordant review. The popper, though, lands ever-so-delicately above a submerged brush pile and just alongside a pad of green ooze. I'm in bass heaven for sure. Immediately I detect a nearby disturbance. Someone's taken notice, someone who may be on in years. A quick slurp and I'm involved with a good fish.

Unfortunately, my identification of the submerged brush pile occurred after my cast or was lost in my zeal for finding fish. Either way, I've got to deal with the second part of the hook-catch equation. The bass is keenly aware of my precarious situation, as all bass are in their infinite wisdom. He could head in any number of directions but instead sums up his options for escape in a split-second and makes a bee-line for the brush, without even the requisite jump. I realize that there's no way I can tow in a 10-pound combination of bass and branches with what I've got for equipment. Maybe next time I'll cast some wire from atop one of the caterpillars.

I get as close as possible to the source of the problem and end our brief relationship with a sharp jerk to the line. There's some consolation, from a standpoint of guilt, that my prey had already escaped scot-free. I was doing battle with a clump of firewood. My popper smiles up at me from a slimy and temptingly-near twig which, now that it's free of my line, looks as though it could be snapped in two by a stiff breeze. I don't care, I've got plenty of reinforcements, and there are plenty more bass, bigger bass. I'm sure of it.

The light is starting to fade in my shady thicket, although sunset won't officially occur for another half-hour. I'm starting to grow a little impatient, as evidenced by my fumbled attempts at threading another popper. "Okay," I say, starting a dialog with myself as I often do when being taunted by the fish-gods, "How about I don't use another popper? You happy now? I'll use something else, is that what you want?" No response, only crow amusement, as I sarcastically produce and display a homemade blob of yellow fur with some black feathers poking out in all directions. Bass are not picky, especially at this dimly-lit hour. I could probably tie on a piece of the slimy twig and get a reaction. What the heck.

With the yellow blob secured, I reprise my symphony in reverse, the fly landing to my right and near another juicy ooze pad. Nothing! Maybe the hairy, furry thing crossed the line into absurdity. Suddenly, out toward the middle, the placid surface is broken by what sounds like a bowling ball dropping from the sky. I study the explosion to see if a duck emerges. Or maybe a water rat or snapping turtle, I've spotted both here before. Seconds pass with no curtain call. There can be only one other explanation, and I'm getting increasingly excited about it. The problem is how, from my current location and position, am I going to make it out that far. I take a look around and realize that while the brush is pretty thick, the branches themselves aren't. During my youth I spent a lot of time landscaping, and in a single day my cronies and I could turn an overgrown property into a manicured showpiece. I start frantically breaking off as much as I can, using some rough but effective approximations of my old methods. A minute later I've hollowed out enough space to perform a forward roll cast, if I wade in to the edge of the drop-off. The question is, what's Mr. Bowling Ball been doing in the meantime? As if in response, there's another equally enormous explosion in the vicinity of the first. He's still there and he's still hungry, or pissed off, or both. I might suspect that it's a carp, they've fooled me on many occasions, but I'm relatively certain there are no carp in either of these quarries.

I slide out into the shallow water and get as close to the drop-off as caution will allow. After a near-death experience with a snapping turtle during my formative years, in which I literally had my finger in the mouth of a 3-footer, I am extremely squeamish about swimming in freshwater. This water holds snapping turtles, though it's not all that fresh.

My enthusiasm over the matter at hand overrides any trepidation. I perform a series of rolls and get the fur ball clear of shore yet short of the disturbance. Because of its size that's the best I can expect. The fly rests motionless. Five seconds go by. The fly rests motionless. Movement is not always important, especially on the surface, or even underwater in some cases. Bass tend to be impulsive, but they are also given to periods of profound thought as they size up a late supper. Another ten seconds. He may have gotten his fill from whatever brought him to the surface moments before. Or perhaps I missed the nightly deadline while busy with my spur-of-the-moment landscaping project.

The water erupts in a tremendous boil. A bass the type of fables surely does live here, and by God he's got a taste for some yellow fuzz. My line doesn't move too much, and in the vanishing light I can't see what's become of the fly. It appears to be missing, but he could have taken it under and then spit it out. With conditions as they are at the shore, I can't easily pull back to set the hook. I've never been one to lay into a big set anyway. I've got to wait and let the tension build at the other end, if it exists at all. The line starts slowly moving, ever-so-slowly, then starts taking off! He's on there, all right, at least for now. I let him take out the slack and then I pull the rod sideways, barely clearing the underside of the thicket. Got him!

This is an enormous fish. The drag screams and I glance nervously at the McMansion. I consider where he might go to get out of this predicament. Other than the brush pile, there are no visible water hazards–the lily pads, stumps and boulders that frustrate fishermen the world over. Still, anything's possible until we're up close and personal.

I maintain constant but courteous resistance and let him roam around for awhile, each second lasting a minute. Then the line starts coming up. A jumping bass is a thing of beauty, but oftentimes, sadly, the first and last eye-to-eye meeting. I keep the rod down in a vain attempt to discourage such unruly behavior. He's still coming up and, worse, he's coming toward me at the same time. Another aquatic Aristotle, just my luck.

He reaches the surface and launches into mid-air directly in front of me. He's got to be twice the size of anything I imagined was residing here. If I'd known about him I would have adjusted my tackle accordingly. Leaders are kept elegantly thin until an experience like this one, after which they become thick and clumsy, but

strong, until the catches dwindle. Next time I'll be ready. For now, I've got to be careful. The jump is complete, the worst is over and somehow he's still on there. But wait, he's headed for the brush pile! I furiously retrieve the slack as he moves to my left. He's not tired yet but has slowed enough to be dissuaded from his woodland destination. Back to the right and out again. This guy's never felt a hook before and is clearly no fan of the shore.

After five minutes he's spent, I'm spent, and in he comes. I grab his lower lip and lift him up in classic form. What a beauty. A solid six pounds and not an ounce of fat. He looks to be about two feet long. I spend a moment with him. He looks at me, wondering about my intentions. I commend him on a fine battle. Then I ease him into the shallow water, leading him along to reacquaint him. This is what it's all about, the reward for all my patience and perseverance, not to mention my soaked attire, scratched arms and missing tackle. At rare times like this I'm actually willing to admit it doesn't get any better, there isn't a bigger fish waiting for my next cast, and it's time to go home and relax.

Subsequent trips to the forbidden quarry have produced a few other prizes. Generally, for whatever reason (possibly because of the vegetation), it seems to have bigger fish. As a result, I have taken it upon myself to institute an informal stocking process, a balancing of riches, so to speak, which involves crossing the 40-foot strip of land with a hefty bass in hand and depositing him in the more accessible quarry. I don't think the bass mind, I suspect even the McMansion folks wouldn't mind, though I forgot to ask their permission. I hear that the quarrymen sometimes wet a line, so why not throw in a surprise or two? I'm willing to share and it's their place too. Just make sure to throw them back, I'm keeping a close watch and it's the right thing to do. After all, one wouldn't want his bulldozer cab to develop a curious "Essence of Rock Bass" aroma.

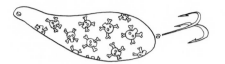

The World's Strongest Bait Bucket

Nukin' 'em at the Boil

By Sebastian O'Kelly

Lots of images come to a mind when people think about nuclear power. Jane Fonda standing by a chained link fence with a bull-horn to her throat. A bunch of raggedy-looking folks with bad B.O. next to her waving signs. Middle-aged white guys with hard hats staring back from the other side of the fence. Giant concrete towers, edifices to man's industrial might, cranking out a gazillion watts of energy. Hazardous waste with no place to go but a hole in the ground somewhere near Vegas. Chernobyl. Three Mile Island. Great fishing.

But wait. I slipped 'great fishing' in there at the end of the para-graph. People don't think of fishing when referring to nuclear power, except maybe to make some joke about fish glowing in the dark.

But it's true (about the great fishing, not the fish glowing in the dark), especially for us brown water fishermen who celebrate the fact that man-made structures–be they power plants, dams, bridges, rock quarries, reservoir spillways, highway ditches, and their artificially-cre-ated mini-ecosystems–can yield some astonishing fishing. Whether these structures create a net positive for the environment and, in the case of a number of dams, should remain, is up to the experts to decide. In the meantime, we'll fish them where we can and in our own way and let Jane and the hard hats yell at each other over the fence.

Which is what my friends Rich, Steph (names slightly altered for lawsuit protection) and I were doing (both fishing and yelling at each other) on a gorgeous June day in the middle of the Chesapeake Bay. We had hired a guide with a boat (Okay, this is a deviation from the offbeat fishing way of self-reliance but being boat-less on the Chesapeake is like being 18 all over again and not having any wheels.) and knocked work into the next day. In the morning, we ran over to the Eastern Shore and tried some of the shallow cuts and back bays flowing through verdant and undeveloped wetlands. We started out on the short sticks and planned to move up to the long wands as the day and fishing progressed. We managed a few small stripers before the sun edged up and the fishing slowed to a caterpillar crawl. The quiet beauty of the place made up for the sluggish fishing, at least for a little while.

We had high expectations for this trip. Late last fall, Rich and I took Steph and some others eeling for big cow stripers in the rips off of Cape May, N.J.–about as sure-fire a guarantee at catching a big bass that you'll get. Unfortunately, that day we faced a howler out of the Northeast and the fishing was slow despite the involuntary contributions to the chum slick by a number of the fishermen. Rich and I each caught a nice fish, Steph caught none. So he got skunked.

Actually, he caught a whelk. I'd never heard of a whelk being caught on a rod and reel before, so we introduced a new word into the fishing lexicon–"whelked." Steph got whelked. At the end of the day, Rich kindly packed one of his bass fillets into a cooler for Steph and

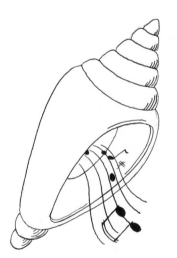

nestled the whelk next to it. It rests somewhere on Steph's cabinet by his bed. When his girlfriend holds it to her ear and says she can hear the ocean, Steph can proudly say that he battled 8-foot swells to catch that whelk.

This trip he was determined to get neither skunked nor whelked, although after popping his second Coors before 11 am he might have been aiming for a similar sounding word. Steph was whizzing casts with enthusiasm, a rubber Bass Assassin clinging to a jig head for dear life, as his casts went in every which direction but the intended one and in no way could be called easy on the eyes, lure, water, or side of the boat–which was picking up dings here and there much to Captain Darren's chagrin. Steph was a stand-up guy and an avid fisher (just not the most experienced one) and greeted his haphazard casts with alternating curses and wisecracks. He was having fun but his eyes were beginning to take on that haunted look of "been there before, here we go again," especially after Rich and I had already caught a few.

Rich, on the other hand, was pursuing his quarry with the studied detachment of a scientist, flicking expert casts that landed inches from the bank, counting down until the jig hit bottom then retrieving it with a pause and twitch before sending another cast out just a couple feet down the bank from the previous one and repeating the drill. Rich actually has a graduate degree in marine biology supplemented by real-life experience as a mate on a New Jersey party boat while growing up, and as a netter for the state of North Carolina performing inshore fish counts. In the office where we work, he is often called Nature Boy, but usually not to his face as he can sometimes be tightly-wound (though the opposite while at play). He can tell you the type of mountain laurel that grows in the Shenandoah, describe the migratory patterns of the grosbeak, and identify the age of a snook by examining its inner ear. He is also a very good fisherman.

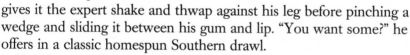

Steph pulls a can of dip from his back pocket and gives it the expert shake and thwap against his leg before pinching a wedge and sliding it between his gum and lip. "You want some?" he offers in a classic homespun Southern drawl.

I shake my head. I could already feel the hot sun sucking the moisture from my body without adding the dehydrating effects of chewing tobacco. Ditto for Coors. I could see the back of Steph's neck reddening. "I've got some sunscreen if you'd like. Your neck's getting fried already."

"Naw," he replies. "I'm either red or pasty white–there ain't no in-between." He reaches for his cap and turns it around to where the University of Maryland Terrapin faces backwards. "Instant sun protection."

I laugh. "Maybe now your luck will turn around also." Like me, Steph shaves his head, a victim of preemie baldness. No Rogaine, Propecia, or other follicular snake oil for either of us though.

"It's my lucky cap. The Terps, baby. This year's NCAA champs. Love them turtles." He grins before shooting a wad of spit into the water near me. It's the third time today that he has reminded me, a Duke graduate, of that fact.

"Tobacco juice has been known to attract whelks," I say.

"I guess I oughta spit more your way then." He pulls a chunk of weeds from his hook. The veneer of bravura fades and his true feelings come forth. "Aw, don't say that. I gotta get on the board here. All I'm gettin' is weeds."

The sun moves up higher and it's clear that most fish in the shallows have moved into deeper water or under cover. Then Steph finally gets his fish, a smallie striper that hit off of a point. He reels it in with gusto, his hand jerking the handle in fits and starts and horsing it home, thinking the fish might get off at any moment. The boy is damn determined not to get skunked this time. There is a lot of hooting and hollering and high fives all around. You would have thought the striper was forty inches, not fourteen.

With his tobacco chewing, boisterous enthusiasm, and down home style, Steph presents himself as an outdoor everyman looking for fun in the sun. It's a little bit of a false image though. Steph is no Georgia boy–he grew up in the Maryland suburbs. So the accent is a trifle affected, but a necessary job requirement in working for a Congressman from North Carolina whose constituents are not going to be pleased to hear a Yankee voice on the other end of the line when they are petitioning their representative to sponsor a resolution calling October "Descendants of Confederate Soldiers Month." Steph is also no rube. You don't get or keep a job as an aide to a Congressman without at least one college degree and decent book and people smarts. So the country boy approach to things is something of a shtick for Steph even if it does reflect some of his true bent.

"Let's reel up guys," Darren says, his tanned face, designer outerwear dress shirt, and polarized Wayfarers the picture of guide cool. "We'll head back across the Bay and try the Boil."

"The Boil?" Nature Boy replies. "Sounds kind of gross." Rich is also a neat freak. He is 40 years old, single, fanatical about cleanliness, a lover of fine wine, cats, beautiful birds and classical music. Actually, it's not what you think. Or go ahead and think it, then take it up with his girlfriend, Andrea.

Steph reels his Bass Assassin all the way to where it catches in the top guide. The plastic is torn from the vigor of his casts. He puts a forefinger in his mouth and flicks the used chaw into the water. "Sounds like my kind of place."

Darren bounces us across the Bay. It is one of those hot, clear days with a wind blowing from the South, kicking up waves high enough to give us a rolling ride with enough spray to persuade us to move to the back of the skiff once Darren gets it up on a plane. Just when we're getting tired of the taste of salt in our mouths, he trims the engine and idles her close to the Calvert Cliffs Nuclear Power Plant.

The appearance of the plant is not what you'd expect. There are no

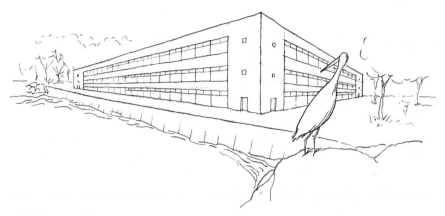

visible giant funnels opening to the sky like those famous pics of Three Mile Island. Instead, a large flat glass building looms impassive just up from the shoreline with some smaller buildings to the left . It looks not unlike some research facility at a university. Running down from its foot to the edge of the water is a massive concrete abutment, presumably a guard against heavy storms and erosion. There are no signs of human activity and the land around it lies undeveloped and unspoiled. It looks peaceful almost.

But inside it is anything but. A huge pipe on the Bay bottom sucks thousands of gallons of saltwater, not to mention more than a few critters, into its giant maw and sends the water rushing in a raging torrent where it is funneled into massive cooling tubes. Atoms ping-ping in an electron slam dance inside a giant mosh pit of a caldron, egged on by pencil eraser-sized pellets of uranium, each with the equivalent energy of a ton of coal. Giant cadmium rods try to maintain order but the atoms have their way, splitting this way and that and generating molten heat. Water bubbles and spits, roils and boils, steams and vents and sends spinning a giant whirly-gig of a turbine that spews electricity so that Baltimore Gas & Electric's customers can turn on their TVs when they get home. The nuclear waste gets farted out the back end into some kind of holding tank. The Bay water acts as the cop at the party, trying to cool everything off–those unruly atoms really get everyone steamed!–so it doesn't all blow to high heaven. Then that cop leaves through an outtake pipe a little bit hot himself, several degrees warmer than the surrounding water. It is an exercise in controlled explosives management. An oxymoron if there ever was one.

We've found the Boil. It looks as its name suggests, water bubbling up seemingly out of nowhere a little ways from shore where the outtake pipe ends somewhere underneath us. Actually, a better description would be the mirrored effect of what you get when you hold a running hose just under water and point it up at an angle. Tendrils of current flick and swirl as a large mass of moving water fans out in a V like a beam from a flashlight that gradually peters out after 200 yards. It is like a river, the effect odd though as it flows through a body of fairly still water, with pockets and seams along the edge presenting nice hidey spots for fish. The turbulent water kicks up organic matter and plankton which attract baitfish and then their predators to feed on the passing meal and inhale the oxygen enriched H_2O. There must be a smorgasbord of goodies that pile out of the pipe too—blue crabs battered from rattling around the pipes; bay anchovies, silversides and menhaden made sluggish from the sudden temperature change and vulnerable to marauding blues, stripers and sea trout; and various worms, annelids, sponges and other prehistoric creatures rudely sucked up from their resting places in the Bay bottom and spat out into the cafeteria food line.

All these factors make for a great fishing spot. Captain Darren tells us that the best time is really in the winter and early spring, where the temperature difference attracts fish like winter skiers to a warming blaze on the hearth. Big stripers stack up in the Boil like logs in a cord of wood, offering light tackle types the best chance to catch a bruiser bass comparable to those that are caught on a more regular basis in the waters off New York, New Jersey and New England. Unfortunately, by this time of year, all those big boys and girls have fled north for the summer. But left behind are many of the younger generation for us to cast to.

The Boil isn't exactly a secret and on the weekends it can get jammed with boats. There is an informal etiquette to fishing it. You are supposed to motor up alongside of the moving water to the top, wait your turn, then shoot in after giving the boat in front ample space to drift and cast. The engine should be turned off or set to a low idle as you drift down the water and fish. Once the Boil tails out, you power back up to the top and drift through it again. The process gets very interesting when there are a couple dozen boats shouldering their way into position. Inevitably, there is some gunwale bumpin' 'n' grinding and tempers start to get on edge. Then some yahoo will cut the line or, worse, anchor in the middle of the drift, or worst of all, troll right across the Boil, big planer boards digging into the water and either slicing or

snagging the lines of those playing by the rules. Tempers blow, curses and middle fingers fly, heavy engine revving starts, and the surf rods come out as heavily trebled plugs are launched at the offending boat. The fishing karma is now upset and a number of folks two-stroke it out of there in fuel-injected anger to fish elsewhere.

Luckily, it is a weekday and only two other boats are here. Two old-timers are fishing cut bait in a Sea Ray anchored by the top of the Boil. At least they are out of the drift. Another boat is floating its way down, the rods of both anglers bent. Steph points them out and Rich and I smile. The Boil is looking very good as Darren maneuvers us into position.

"Do you mind if I give the fly rod a shot?" I ask Darren. He hands me a rod ready to go with a Clouser tied on. It has a shooting head and fast taper and I'm quickly booming out double-hauls of almost Rajeffian distance, a marked contrast from my usual middle management-type casts on lesser equipment. One of my shots reaches across the water flow and lands near the anchored boat, startling the old-timers with their pool stick poles that can't cast much farther than they can see, which is about far enough to see impending roadkill while behind the wheel. I offer them a friendly wave which they acknowledge. Looks like their eyesight is better than I thought, and their fishing skills too as one of them rears back to set a hook.

"This is some rod," I say. It's nice to have the light feel of the fly rod in my hand after casting heavily-weighted Bass Assassins all morning. I take care to avoid tangling the others, always a challenge with Steph's whirly-bird casts. The wind, plus the boat twisting and turning in the current as it drifts, makes it tough.

"It's the new T-3 from Orvis," Darren answers. "She throws a lot of line."

On my second cast, I get a hit on the strip back and feel that familiar but always welcome strain in my forearm. The fish isn't big enough to get on the reel so I strip it in, the current adding a few extra inches to the fight. I hear a yell next to me and I don't have to look over to see who else has hooked up. Then Rich nails a fish.

"Triple header," Darren cries. We land our fish as we tail out of the Boil. They are thick, spunky stripers, "schoolies" as they are referred to in the vernacular. Darren motors us back up to the top. Steph has high-fived everyone at least twice by the time we get there.

We catch fish on every drift. There are no bruisers, but they have

enough pull that the thin running line on Darren's rod starts rubbing my index finger red. Steph's enthusiasm is infectious and everyone is jumping up and shouting with every fish, even when a dink is brought to the side. I'm matching fish for fish with the long wand against the short sticks. I might even be a little ahead—I always take quiet satisfaction on those occasions of being able to out-perform the spin crowd and defy traditional theory which holds that lures or bait are always better than flies, excepting when angling for insect-eating trout. The action slows a little—the sun is now at high noon—and I rest for moment. Nature Boy has stopped too and is sizing up some blue herons along the shoreline with his binoculars. The Plant sits on over 2,000 undeveloped acres and is home to a cornucopia of wildlife—ospreys, bald eagles, herons, deer, foxes, racoons and other critters. It would probably come as a surprise to some that the Plant owners have an agreement with the Nature Conservancy to set aside a certain amount of land to protect the endangered tiger beetle, which likes to traipse about the place without regard to the high-level nuclear waste stored in (supposedly) secure holding tanks. The irony of such wildlife teeming around a facility which, if something went drastically wrong, could annihilate all living creatures within a 10 mile radius is not lost on me.

I offer the fly rod to Steph. He is so fired up that he looks like he will take it. But then he pauses and goes quiet for the first time since we got to the Boil. He hesitates, his eyes flickering with doubt, then says he is having too much fun with the Bass Assassin.

I wonder why he backed off—was it that fear that many newbies have of this buggy whip rod and floppy line flying every which way but where you want it to go? Maybe it is hearing a lot of daunting technical jargon said about things like "weight forward" which could reasonably be interpreted as the position you are to be in when casting rather than what it really means–the taper of the fly line. If we are to get technical and really scare off the inexperienced, how about throwing around some of the Latin names given to the insects flies represent? *Leptophlebia cupida*, for example. To the lay person, that might sound like the latest STD making the rounds in the singles' scene. Imagine telling the new female fly fisher that she must put one in her box and just watch her reaction! What about chironomid for that matter? Is that a term for a new kind of worm infecting the hard drives of PCs across America? All the technical terminology associated with fly fishing can be absolutely intimidating to the uninitiated.

I wonder if there is another factor behind Steph's reluctance. Could it have to do with my pet theory–that a social, cultural and economic divide exists between spin and fly fishermen. Perhaps something clicked deep within his subconscious about not wanting to cross that divide by picking up the fly rod? Who knows? I know I'm getting a little heavy here. I'm also generalizing. But while there are certainly those who cross back and forth between the two realms, there is most definitely such a divide between those who predominantly spin fish and those who fly fish.

I've often wondered why the fly fishing industry hasn't done more to breach this divide. The Stephs of the world, often called the hook and bullet crowd by the industry, are a huge untapped demographic segment and market for the fly fishing companies. But this demographic also represents something of a dilemma. While your typical hook and bulleter may plunk down $250 for a laser-guided paint gun, it's doubtful he will fork over $1,000 for a Sage rod and Abel reel. He could go for the $89 Cabela cheapo combo and risk having it break with the first good fish, but he's too smart for that and quality does count for him. So the margins would have to come down on fly fishing equipment without a significant degradation in performance. Some of the companies are moving in that direction but aren't there yet.

The economics could be taken care of, but there is still that social and cultural divide. It's the difference between wanting to hop on a plane to Paris, France to see a new exhibition of nudes at the Louvre and climbing in your truck to drive to Paris, Texas to see the real thing at the Lover Bar. There are other analogies–*USA Today* versus the *New York Times*, blackjack versus bridge, gun ownership versus gun control, and so forth. Again, I am generalizing quite a bit, but you get the point.

To go along with a downsizing in price, a shift in marketing might help bridge this divide. Imagine the following broadcast at Daytona: "Brett Bodine is leading down the backstretch but Ricky Rudd in the Orvis Car is gaining fast and reeling in cars, one by one." Or how about Mark McGuire on TV with a fly rod clutched in one of his tackle box-sized fists: "For your everyday fly fishing needs, I recommend the Loomis Z-6000. It casts long"–cut to him crushing a baseball with a mighty swing–"but lands soft"–cut to him hugging his son after he broke the home run record. Lastly, if you got Roland Martin to wave a fly rod around for a couple of his fishing shows, that would move scads of folks to add a long wand next to their dozen bait-casters in the basement locker.

Would those marketing approaches attract "hook and bulleters" to the sport? Without a doubt, in my mind. Then why aren't the fly fishing tackle companies making them? I think in a lot of ways they prefer that the divide remain intact. High-end products and elite imagery, sprinkled with a dose of mysticism and escapism, are what attracts much of their current customer base and enables those high margins. Expanding the demographic reach is too great a risk of losing buyers who like to separate themselves from the rest. Ask a few fly fishermen in a derisive mood after a few beers what they think of spin fishermen and you get "worm dunkers," "meat fishermen," and sometimes "rednecks." Ask the converse and you might get a response about lack of manhood and sexual preferences. That's when the lines separating the two glows a little more brightly.

I know this isn't the case with every fisherman, fly or spin. And there are a number of those within the fraternity who come from modest means. But these generalizations do hold some truth and it's a real shame in my view–fly fishing could significantly benefit from

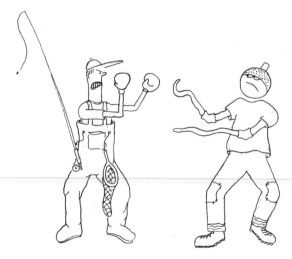

greater diversity. The more, the merrier, just as long as no one fishes where my friends and I go. But I imagine that it is the following night-mare scenario, exaggerated of course, that lurks in the back of the fly fishing company chiefs when they make their business decisions.

It is a beautiful August evening at Buffalo Ford on the Yellowstone River in the Park. Anglers are spread evenly along its stretch, each minding the others' space. The pace of fishing is deliberate and stud-ied at this well-known spot where the fish have Ph.Ds in fly identifi-cation. Caddis are starting to come off and the cutts, abandoning their daytime wariness, are slashing at the fluttering insects, their splashes breaking the glassy surface. The sun glows orange and cool air settles with just the whisper of a breeze.

This reverie is broken with the sound of spitting gravel and the roar of a 427 cubic inch engine with bored out headers as a flame orange 1980's Camaro with a black eagle spread on the hood pulls in. The car's bumpers are festooned with stickers about the right to bear arms. Out steps a young man with heavy peach fuzz on his lip and a black Iron Maiden t-shirt. He sports a mullet cut with a rat-tail and a dia-mond stud in one ear.

His girl emerges from the driver side, yellow, Jersey-style hair piled up on her head, prime material for tying a Brooks Blonde streamer given its stiff waterproofed finish thanks to the latest in hair care prod-ucts. She's wearing a fuchsia tube top that just isn't up to the task of supporting a pair of heavy breasts–the size of a couple of Alaska rain-bows–that have already felt the tug of many hands in their young lives. Written across the front of her top are the words–"It's the Size of the Boat AND the Motion in the Ocean." A pair of tight, low-hipped jeans cover a pair of legs with the length and taper of a Loomis 10-weight. Between the two pieces of clothing is a wide expanse of skin highlight-ed by a belly ring. Right above the pant button lies a tattoo of a preen-ing mongoose with the letters S-N-A-K-E-A-T-E-R emblazoned next to it.

The young man hitches his rubber hip boots to his cut-offs and strings up his rod, tying on a large grasshopper imitation that he bought at a fly shop in Livingston because it looked super realistic and because its hook eye was big enough to tie directly to the leader, which is quite thick as the result of break offs from a trip the day before (he hasn't yet learned of the benefit of tippet material). He motions to the girl to leave both doors open and turn up the stereo before he half-wades, half-stumbles to an open spot in the river. His casts are a little clumsy but he has most of the basics down and there is some sense of fishing instinct in his hands and the way he follows his drift downstream with his rod-tip. The symphonic sound of crickets in

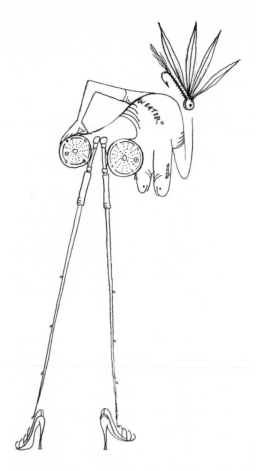

the anglers' ears is soon displaced by the heavy guitar riffs of ZZ Top's "Tube Snake Boogie." No sweet melody of nature wafts across the water on this fine summer's eve, but rather the Texas rasp and twang of one of Southern rock's all-time bests.

I got a girl, she lives on the hill.
She won't do it but her sister will,
When she boogie,
She do the tube snake boogie.
Well now boogie little baby,
Boogie woogie all night long...

Back at the car, her hip cocked at a provocative angle and dragging on a Marlboro Light, the girl is shouting encouragement to her man and makes a little bunny hop and high-pitched yelp when, incredibly, he hooks a decent-sized cutthroat that somehow mistakes his grasshopper for the world's largest caddis. He lands the fish quickly, inserting a finger under the gill cover to quiet its wriggle while wresting free the barbed hook. With the other hand he raises the rod butt and deals a death blow across the fish's head. He pulls a supermarket baggy from his rear pocket, wraps the cutt, and knots it to a belt loop (he hasn't yet learned the benefit of catch and release, nor compliance with the Park's strict conservation regulations, and he looks as if he cares not to).

This last act is too much for about a dozen anglers and, en masse, they trudge in a line toward the bank, tight-lipped and heads down

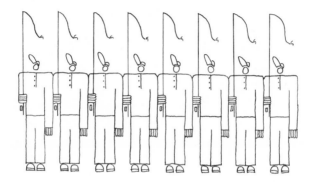

only to look up as they pass the girl to sneak a peak at her jiggling 'bows that seem to be keeping their own beat to ZZ Top. She wags her tongue at them and the dying rays of the sun glint silver off the stud in her mouth, which upon closer inspection is a dead ringer for a pair of Clouser dumbbell eyes. The men return to their cars and wordlessly pack up their rods, vowing never to fly fish again. As they drive off in the latest SUVs, they start thinking of other hobbies to take up–lawn bowling, polo, truffle hunting come to mind–where they will never have to cross paths again with people like the two they just left behind.

My editorializing and overly-active imagination are disturbed by a shout from a familiar voice. Steph's onto another fish. He plays and handles it with confidence he did not have in the morning, even unhooking it himself. He holds the fish up, a nice 20-incher.

"That's my best fish today," he says. It's keeping size under the Bay's paltry 18 inch minimum, but Steph releases it. Putting fish in the box is not the goal of this trip.

"It sure beats catching a whelk," Rich remarks.

"That it does." Steph lifts his cap to wipe the sweat off his shiny dome. There is a pink shadow line signifying the edge of the cap. "We sure are nukin' 'em at the Boil."

Steph spoke too soon, violating the fishermen's pledge–albeit oft-broken–of celebrating the success of a spot while in the midst of its action. So the fish shut down. We drift a few more times through the Boil without any luck before Darren has us reel up. We motor a short way to another spot along the shoreline that I call Crab Pot City for its plethora of buoy-marked pots and go back to jigging with the short sticks. The action is slow, although Rich does land the best fish of the day.

By now, the combination of an early a.m. wakeup, 8 hours of hot sun, lots of fishing, and no fuel in the belly since breakfast has worn us down. Darren ferries us back to the marina. Thanks and high fives are exchanged, plus promises to do it again. Steph, Rich and I wolf our lunch down while sitting on the dock, barefoot with rolled-up pants and legs hanging over the side like a Huck Finn painting, and talk about how a nuclear power plant turned an average day of fishing into an excellent one.

Now that Ted has kicked Jane off his ranch and out of his Braves

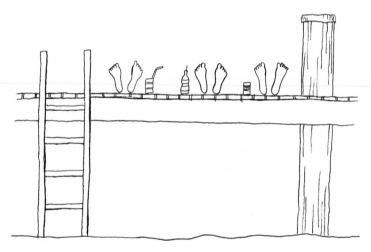

skybox, maybe she will take up anti-nuke activism again. Hopefully, their break up and Ted's love of fishing will not spawn in her a knee-jerk reaction to stop all fishing too. Good luck. Stick to the nukes would be my advice on that score. She can hook up with all her old friends with the B.O., plus some of their offspring fresh off of an effort to shut down the World Bank, and take up the bullhorn outside the gate across from the old guys in hard hats who wish America was still the way it was back in the 1950s. They will have at it with no accommodation in sight.

As for me, I'll leave the protests to Jane and her friends. Steph (with the short stick) and I (with the long wand), and maybe Nature Boy too, will be on the other side of the plant fishing. We'll have a healthy respect for each other's tackle and way of fishing. And we will be nukin' 'em at the Boil.

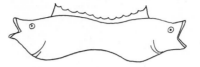

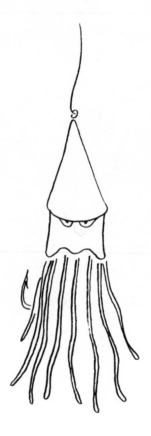

Get Jiggy with the Squiddy!

Ode to the Bobber

By Christopher Arelt

What light from yonder lakefront burns?
Is it our fair sun come arisen on morning hillcrest?
No, it is the bobber.

There's a time for lures and a time for flies,
A time for craft and a time for stealth,
But when you've tried too many tries,
Are failing in your fishing health,
Make your way to a local tackle shop.

Or Wal-Mart as your spirit Lowe's,
Set your sights on a Target round,
For there you'll find in the angling rows,
Bobbers selling by the pound,
Beside the latest gimmick crop.

Chug-bait, crank-bait, flatfish, bug,
Hula-poppers and atomic ants,
Ol' bucket-mouth, he'll laugh and shrug,
Then mutter how you stood no chance,
And wait for something real.

So pass by this the latest fare,
And make your way to the plastic spheres,

Red and white all waiting there,
To elevate you 'bove your peers,
As they watch your mono peel.

The price is right so don't delay,
No need for makeshift cork or spool,
"Strike indicator" some might say,
to euphemize this simple tool,
Which signals something's there.

Your prize in hand at register,
You seem a little circumspect,
A thing of such diameter,
Might cause another to inspect:
"That ain't no ear of Hare."

Yet back at pondside all is well,
You snap it on and off you go,
A threaded worm, a hook and snell,
A rocket-launching throw,
And pontoon landing near the pads.

Below the surface fish remark,
And gather to review:
"Perhaps there's a new baseball park?"
"No, this is nothing new,"
We've had it with those silly fads.

So one by one they each agree,
Tradition be unswerved,
The biggest one says, "Look at me!"
And dinner has been served,
With a mighty wake indeed.

But lest we think this fishy tale,
Must have a happy ending,
The fisherman is doomed to fail,
Despite his rod a-bending,
As the bobber finds the weed.

Hanging Shads

By Sebastian O'Kelly

I n the fall of 2000, the fate of who would be our President was not
known for several weeks after the November election. It came
down to the proper counting of a few thousand paper ballots cast
in southern Florida. Added to the drama were high-stakes legal
maneuverings on both sides, garrulous political spinmeisters har-
rumphing across the airwaves, and the sight of people peering over
card files that looked to be straight out of the Dewey Decimal System.

A media onslaught rivaling the O.J. trial was sprung upon cable
watchers, newsophiles and other boob tube gazers. Even the political-
ly-oblivious looking for reruns of "Everyone Loves Raymond" couldn't
avoid the non-stop blather of the TV talking heads. New media-gener-
ated personalities burst into America's consciousness whether we wanted them or not. The cognoscenti gave this year's Kato Kaelin award to
a heavily made-up woman in charge of the final vote count. She had a
background in throwing fabulous parties and high society events in her
hometown of Sarasota, which went to show that if you can manage an
accurate guest count of 40 for brunch at the local horticultural society,
it shouldn't be too hard to coordinate counting a few million voters
across the state. Unlike affable, harmless Kato, she did not fade into the
good night but has since parlayed her 15 minutes of fame into a
Congressional seat.

Along the way, some new words and phrases were introduced into the national lexicon—butterfly ballots, hanging chads, pregnant chads, dimpled chads and various other "chads" not of the African country of that name. Ballot punching procedures became a national obsession until finally George W. Bush was declared the winner. As an Al Gore supporter and loyal Democrat, his defeat left an unpleasant taste in my mouth. As a Clinton administration political appointee whose Federal job was determined by what party controlled the Executive Branch, that taste went from unpleasant to bitter as I updated my resume and readied my departure papers. And bitter turned to acid upon the thought that 3,000 other Clintonites would also be joining me, many of us competing for the same types of jobs in a town that had just gone Republican. I was a career cross between a policy wonk and a bureaucrat and feeling none too good about it.

Luckily, before that acid left a permanent burn along my gums and

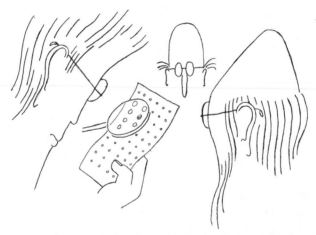

before the unemployment check stubs had piled too high, I found a consulting gig with a small law firm located in Arlington, Virginia (across the Potomac River). The work was flexible, pay decent and boss good. Almost as importantly, I was situated just two miles from what may be the best river for urban fishing in America.

When you tell non-fishing Washingtonians of that fact, you usually get a funny look and maybe a comment about how the Potomac is so polluted that it once caught on fire and that there couldn't possibly be any fish in there and that what few there were would give you cancer after a few meals. They are dead wrong on the first two and mostly wrong on the third, if you believe the fish advisories. The Potomac never caught on fire—that was the Cuyahoga in Ohio over 30 years ago. And while the public health authorities do not recommend consuming Potomac-caught fish, those fish and their watery environ are much cleaner now than they used to be, thanks to stricter government regulations over various sources of pollution.

As for the fishing, you can't find a major river in America that goes through a big city with such prolific and diverse piscatorial opportunities. Less than 100 miles northwest of Washington, the Potomac–its North branch to be exact–has produced state record brown trout as a classic tailwater. Half that distance south of the city, she gives up monster 40-pound stripers and black drum every year. And in parts in-between, she is home, depending on time of year, to stripers, spot, croaker, blues, pickerel, white and yellow perch, herring, bluegill, largemouth and smallmouth bass, carp, tiger muskies, sturgeon, crappie, channel and blue catfish, and hickory, gizzard and American shad, just to name a few.

It is the shad that is the focus of this tale; more specifically, the hickory and their bigger cousin the American–as the other shad species are of little fishing value. Each year during the spring, these anadromous, prehistoric fish make their spawning runs up most of the major rivers on our Eastern seaboard, as well as in a few river systems out West, where they are a species introduced by man. The famous naturalist and writer John McPhee calls them our "Founding Fish" in his book of that name and his title is certainly apt as shad played a role in sustaining our early settlers through those tough winters. They were in fact served as a meal at George Washington's home, Mt. Vernon, located on the Potomac south of the city. To this day, shad pour up many of our major rivers to do their thing each spring and despite excessive pollution, riverside development, deforestation, over-fishing, dams and all manner of traditional obstacles and enemies, they continue to thrive in many rivers with astounding resilience. McPhee could well have called them "Ending Fish" as well, because these tough, fecund fish more than likely will still be swimming long after man is gone from the shores.

As anyone will tell you who has fished for shad, they are tricky fish. One day, they will hit with the aggressive and dim-witted nature of panfish, the next they have no more interest in your offering than the wisest brown trout being shown a giant plug used for marlin. And there are some days when they are a little in the middle. Traditionally, shad are pursued via a jigging motion on light spinning tackle with "shad darts," small rhomboid-shaped jigs on size 4 to 8 hooks, with colors red, yellow, or chartreuse over white. On the long wand, flies of similar size and color are used and retrieved with a strip-and-pause motion.

I think what makes them tricky, especially in these parts, has to do with the time of year they choose to make their spawning runs. That usually is in the fickle month of April. In April, Washington, D.C. can see 85 degree sunny days turn into 50 degree, blustery rainy days and back in the space of a week. And those swings will make water temps jump up and down like nattering journalists seeking recognition at a White House press conference, not to mention cause all sorts of kaleidoscope-like changes in water clarity. Those kinds of rapid changes can throw any fish into a teenaged funk and shad seem to be especially sensitive to them.

Shad are also brown water fish. That is for catching purposes. Not the gloppy, chocolatey, "got the runs" kind (no fish thrives in that color water except for the bottom-hugging catfish), but the milky, slightly brownish-greenish kind. I discovered this to be so just recently one day on Deer Creek, a small tributary of the Susquehanna near Havre de Grace.

It was a drought year, with water levels near record lows. It was actually the second dry year–last year the water was almost as clear and low and the fishing had been fairly poor as opposed to outstanding in previous years where there had been decent run-off giving the creek that rich, milky color. This time, I could see the shad daisy chaining and figure eighting a rod length away, their silver forms skittish and alert, large silver dollar-sized eyes appearing to catch any movement like the Eye of Sauron without the evil intent. The wave of my fly rod would scatter them like cats, the retrieval of my small chartreuse fly tied with sparkly estaz chenille–normally deadly in murkier-watered years–through their midst was akin to tossing a pit bull on top of them until they figured out that the fly would do them no harm, then they ignored it like the fat, pimply girl unexpectedly thrust into the crowd of popular class beauties, sliding sideways a few inches with an indignant flick of the tail if the fly happened to brush against their flanks. After awhile, the thought that these fish could be caught on any fly or lure seemed utterly implausible except for the fact that in years past I had caught them in this very same spot with this very same fly. But after several fruitless hours on the stream that day I almost had to re-convince myself that those moments of 20-inch ocean fish spiraling in the air on the end of my line were not some "big fish" dream that so often fills my head during idle moments.

One thing I knew about the Potomac, cleaned up though it may be, was that it hadn't been clear since the days Chief Potomac himself

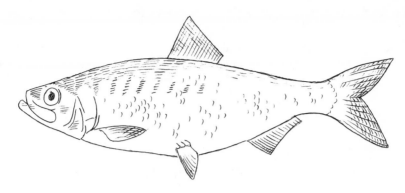

Hickory Shad

prowled its banks. Those clear water issues just wouldn't be a factor–if anything, I had to worry about big spring rains and the water color growing darker than the Senate's own famous bean soup. I had heard it had a pretty decent shad run, aided by recent construction of a fish ladder to get them past Little Falls into prime spawning territory north of the city.

So I cut out for a long lunch on a slow Friday and with rod in hand and some flies stashed in my work bag, snagged a cab into the city. I quickly learned that trusting your cabbie is never a sure thing in this town and I had to steer him across Key Bridge and north on Canal Road to where a small gravel road diverts off to the left. The cab skittered down the gravel road, then moved through a single lane tunnel blasted 150 years ago through solid granite, its interior unlit and walls dripping wet with condensation. The tunnel's ceiling looked low enough to clip a canoe off a big SUV and the cabbie was peering up as if it might fall at any moment.

Then we came out on the other side to a different world than the crowded city we had just come through. The sky opened to a wide river with several boats spread in a line down from a rocky spit that curved downstream. Clearly, the shad's arrival was not entirely a secret. To our left was a wide parking lot and field with picnic tables dotted here and there among small copses of trees. A small, dull green cinder block structure that looked in size to be a cross between a legitimate building and a storage shack stood as headquarters of sorts for passing bikers, hikers, canoeists and, of course, fishermen.

Here was Fletcher's Boathouse–the place whose location left my cabbie befuddled but has been a DC institution for the four generations that the Fletcher family has run it and a refuge for those in the know who seek to angle in the Potomac's fertile waters. The Boathouse, if one can really call it that because it is really far too small to hold any boats, while modestly fitting in the verdant green of early spring, rested in sharp contrast to the hustling modernity of its host city. It was a piece of early 20th century rural Americana defying efforts to remove and replace it with some shop technologically modern and sophisticated to meet all the 21st century outdoorist's acquisitive needs.

The river curled out, wooded on both sides, much thinner and deeper than where most Washingtonians see it crossing the bridges that connect the city to Virginia. A long, floating dock ran parallel to the bank, a row of wooden dories tied loosely to its cleats.

I settled up with the cabbie and walked up to the Boathouse. Ray Fletcher, thin as a West Virginia birch with twang to match, was behind the register, efficiently processing requests for boat rentals and fishing licenses and equipment. He and his brother Joe own the Park Service lease on the property which is part of the Chesapeake and Ohio National Historical Park.

"How are the shad running?" I asked Ray.

"Hickories are moving up pretty good. No sign yet of any Americans."

"Any being taken on the fly rod?"

"Guy was out there this morning. Don't know if he caught any." Ray's tone was short and to the point, but not unfriendly. The shop was cluttered like all shops of its kind invariably are–a stack of papers along the counter; some life jackets piled in the corner; a few rods lined up next to them, shad darts on a cardboard backing tacked on the wall at an odd angle. A cooler stood behind him, stuffed with bait, the hot seller being whole herring that are fished on the bottom for big spawning stripers. Also, hanging on the wall was a mount of the biggest, fattest white perch I had ever seen. A little unusual I thought, sort of like a hunter sending a chipmunk to a taxidermist. But to each their own.

Ray quickly filled out the paperwork for a D.C. fishing license. He wore a light tan collared shirt with the letters 'AFFTA' stitched on the front pocket. AFFTA stands for the American Fly Fishing Tackle Association, the shirt a gift from AFFTA's Washington lobbyist, Jim Range, who is a regular down here. Ray and Joe have clearly picked up on the fly fishing thing and have also gotten hip to new technology, setting up a web site with regular fishing reports just this past year. Lest you still want to think that these are just a couple of country boys lost in the Big City, the Fletcher boys play the D.C. power game of politics as well. Each year around this time, they help Range set up the "Casting Call" where Congressmen, the Secretary of the Interior, and other power players come out for a morning's fly fishing with some of the sport's most famous celebs–Lefty Kreh came one year–followed by smoked shad for lunch and a lot of elbow rubbing where AFFTA can get the assorted muckity mucks' attention on the hot fishery issues of the day.

That playing the power game proved pretty savvy when the Park Service raised questions about the terms of the Fletcher's lease a few years ago. Range, a former counsel to the Senate Majority Leader sprang into action. Calls were made, buttons pushed and chains yanked. The Park Service promptly backed off. Sadly though, when the Fletchers retire, the lease will terminate as it is conditioned upon staying in the family and none of the Fletcher kids want to follow in the footsteps of their fathers. And both Ray and Joe are not young men.

Ray processed my license and slid me a waiver form. "Is your liabilty insurance high?" I asked. I hoped the trial lawyers were too busy taking on McDonalds over fatty foods and hot coffee to notice Fletcher's.

"Too high," he replied, peeling off a carbon copy. "Makes it real tough to run a business." He pointed down to the water. "Life jackets are in the shed, oars in the box next to it. Take whatever boat you want."

As I traipsed down to the dock, I appreciated his informality and the option of consumer choice. If this were some new, slick outfit of an outfitter, I'd probably have to be measured for life jacket size and take a 30-minute boat safety course, not to mention pay three times the price of $20 that the brothers charge for a day rental. I pulled a life jacket from the wall and found a pair of oars in the box with oar locks firmly attached.

On the weekends, there is a crusty old bird named Paula who will set you up with a boat. Rumor has it that she was once homeless, then taken in by a Fletcher's regular to live in a wing of his house and care for an ailing parent. She walks with the stride of a bandy-legged sailor, with ropy, knotted arms from hauling around boats all day and hands yellowed by Potomac mud.

One Saturday, my friend Steve and I came down to rent a boat. I asked Paula for one with a bigger anchor (if you can call a large river rock gift-wrapped with twine an anchor).

"They're all fine," she said. "The size don't matter."

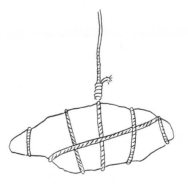

"But you can't go to sea in a canoe," I answered, recalling a closing line from one of my frequent sayings.

"Huh?"

"You know the saying–'It ain't the size of the boat, but the motion in the ocean, but you can't go to sea in a canoe.'"

Her eyes twinkled and she gave us a grey-toothed grin. "I say—'It ain't the heat of the meat, but the angle of the dangle.'" Steve and I chuckled.

She pointed to a coffee can standing on a rock. "That's my retirement fund. They don't pay a pension here." Steve dutifully slipped a dollar inside. On the way back in, she yelled at Steve for navigating us into a concrete piling, the force of which knocked me off my seat and into the bottom of the boat in front of a bunch of people waiting at the dock, the kind of embarrassment that you can't do anything about but laugh at. As a penance for his poor helmsmanship, Paula made Steve put another dollar in her Social Security lockbox.

Still in my work clothes of khakis and a dress shirt, I searched for the driest boat with the biggest rock. The boats were shaped of heavy wood with flat bottoms, a mulish cross between a john boat and a row boat, stable enough to stand and cast from. They were old, plodding, river-worthy craft, horse and buggies to today's sleek, high-performing alloy-formed canoes and kayaks. But they were just fine for Fletcher's and just fine for me.

I maneuvered out from the dock and rowed straight out into the main current, anchoring the boat in a space between about a half dozen others. With nervous hands, I readied my rod, a 5-weight, and attached a reel with 8-weight line. Casting an 8-weight line with such a light rod is not something the fly tackle companies recommend, but I didn't have a fast-sink line in the right size (which was what I needed to get the fly down to the fish in the deep current). 2X served as the tippet—these are strong fish and anything less than 3X will result in a lot of free-swimming shad with your fly nestled in their jaw. I tied on my personal Shad Killer, a fly of my own creation tied with sparkly estaz chenille with Clouser eyes and a yellow marabou tail.

The mother of improvisation trumped the views of the experts once again and I had no problem casting the heavy line. I let it swing downstream in the current and then stripped back once the current formed a "U" in the line. There are many theories as to why shad strike a fly or lure, but the predatory urge is not one as they are filter feeders of plankton, according to McPhee. One theory holds that they strike on their spawning run as part of a protective mechanism against prospective predators of their progeny. I personally think this one is hooey as I have caught shad in the ocean miles and months away from having any urges of parental protection. My own theory is a little more simple and along the lines of "small annoying thing next to me— you piss me off!"

Whatever the theory I was not exactly testing it out with no fish to show after about 15 minutes. I thought I had a strike but that sort of thought can be deceiving when you have not been fishing much recently and are going through a period of "no catching" that extended here after being blanked earlier at Deer Creek. There had been no shads hanging on my line since well-before the 2000 election.

A whoop upstream interrupted my concentration. A large man was deep into a shad, his rod bowed. He wore a dark red shirt and matching shorts with knee-high white socks, burgundy and gold–a die-hard Redskins fan to be sure. He looked up as he pulled the shad into the boat and I gave him a thumbs up and he yelled something down to me. It was the third fish I saw him catch–he'd been into back-to-backs as I rowed out.

Just downstream, a Fletcher's boat was anchored with three older Hispanic men fishing with thick spinning gear. Their lines were taut in the current, bottom-fishing mostly likely for catfish or tasty white perch. Shad are strictly catch and release in the Potomac and as a result, those who fish for the table focus on species like white perch where the bag limits are generous. A mile upstream of us at Chain Bridge where there is ample shore access, you can find lots of Vietnamese, Cambodian, Korean, Mexican and other Hispanic fishermen working the bank on a weekend or weekday evening. Many bring trash cans to load up on the fish and anything caught, regardless of size or species, gets thrown in. I remember reading last year about how fisheries enforcement did a sweep one evening and busted over a hundred people for fishing without licenses. In our earlier days, Chris and I might have been among them.

South of the three men, a dad and his son were also bait fishing. Earlier, the son had landed a nice-sized channel cat. It was a scene one day I hope to play out when my kids are old enough. Below them, there were a couple more boats that I couldn't make out in any detail. It was then I saw that they were all in a straight line anchored at the edge of the current and it was I, the proverbial nail sticking out, being the kink in the line. While the offbeat creed celebrates fishing differently from others, it does not endorse non-conformism for the sake of non-conformism, which is its own perverted brand of conformism, particularly when there is no fish-catching being experienced by one of its adherents. I promptly upped anchor and edged the boat back into a seam right below the 'Skins fan.

It was the right move. On the third cast, the line stopped and I felt the heavy throb of a shad on the other end. It peeled line heading upstream. Occasionally, a hooked shad will turn and head downstream after being hooked–those are the times that they will take you into your backing–but most of the time the homing instinct is so strong that a mere hook and line is not going to dissuade them from continuing their mission. The shad dug hard, shaking its head. Some call shad the "poor man's tarpon" or "mini-tarpon" in describing their fighting ability. The two species are members of the same family and bear a strong resemblance, though I hadn't yet caught a tarpon so I couldn't truly compare their fighting skills. However, I do know if you tied a shad and trout of the same size together tail-to-tail, the shad would tow the trout around well-past the point of saying "Uncle."

I brought the shad in, a bright hickory in the mid-teens inchwise. I lipped the fish to admire it, acknowledged the congratulatory whoop and thumbs up from my upstream friend, and released the shad. Discerning the difference between a hickory and an American is not always easy. Americans are typically bigger, a little more white in color with more of an oval shape, but a big hickory running 20 inches can fool you into thinking he's something he's not. Probably the easiest way to tell is by looking at the lips. Hickories have an underslung jaw like their cousin the tarpon, while the lips on an American come together evenly.

I caught five more shad over the next half hour, all hickories of about the same size, before sitting down to eat a sandwich. The wind had picked up now, but the sun stayed out and kept me from getting cold on a type of day that could keep you pulling a sweater on and off several times throughout its course. As I'm prone to when I'm out on the water not actually fishing, my mind wandered.

I wondered if the new occupant of the White House knows about Fletchers and the fishing here, less than four miles from where he now lives. Does he know of the legions of shad that make their way north in the Potomac each spring? Does he know of the river's tree-lined banks, boulder-strewn bottom, and relative pristine setting, all within Washington's borders? I had heard George W. liked to fish for large-mouths on a number of ponds on his sprawling ranch in Texas (Think of how big those bass must be with the Secret Service stopping any-one trying to fish for them! But this is one set of ponds that somehow Chris and I would not be willing to push past the "No Trespassing" signs for). Perhaps the new President would appreciate the down-home, informal style of the Fletcher operation, given the image he portrays as a country man.

It was then I realized that I was now tasting the sweet instead of the bitter. If the election had turned out differently, right now I'd be running around that giant, decrepit, rat warren of a building called the Commerce Department. I'd be shunting from one meeting to the next, blurry faces around tables in airless, windowless rooms; cranking out memos filled with bureaucratese and obfuscatory language; dodging from cubbyhole to cubbyhole; and pouring over the fine print of some regulation in the Federal Register understood by few and mattering to even less. One thing was for sure. It's doubtful I would be experiencing this wonderful fishery.

The boss's benevolence would last for only so long. I finished my lunch, upped anchor and headed shoreward, exchanging a final thumbs up with my upstream friend. I had caught six fish. Exactly six, proving that I could count shads better than the afore-referenced Florida official.

I peered over the shoulder at the Boathouse as I rowed in. It would be a damn shame if Fletcher's fell one day to "progress" – the Park Service replacing it with some new operation sponsoring eco-friendly, non-invasive nature tours on unsinkable, kevlar-coated canoes where fishing would be prohibited because of harm to the animals. Or just as bad, removing all trace of man at the behest of some well-intentioned but misguided environmental group and re-establishing the area with grasses and shrubs native to the region in the 18th century.

Until then, I would keeping coming back to Fletcher's and hanging shad, fish-willing, and keeping score for this find of a fishery that now counted for me.

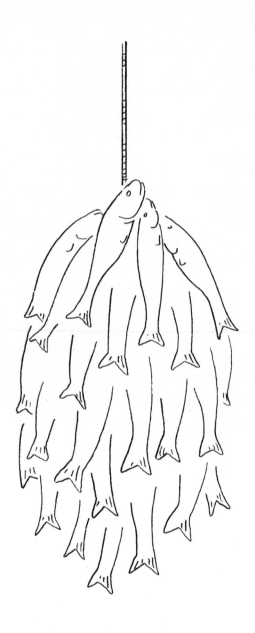

The Days Before Catch and Release

ISO Other Offbeat Anglers

By Sebastian O'Kelly

C hris and I often wonder if there are others out there who sub-
scribe to the offbeat angling creed, other brown water types
who are willing to clamber over that big boulder to explore
parts of a river that most are not willing to prospect, to stop by the
side of a busy road to venture a cast into some forgotten, goop-filled
pond, or to cast a proverbial Bluefish Saltwater Special into a slow run
where everyone else is fishing #24 midges.

Of course, we recognize that taking the offbeat approach isn't
always the best approach to fishing success. That scramble over the
boulder–if you don't wind up with a severe ankle sprain in the process
–could lead to a shallow, riffled section of the river where only mad
toms and sculpins play. The only trophy in that goop-filled pond might
be some grossly-distorted superhero, last year's hot toy discarded in
anticipation of the next plasticine product turned out by the Great
American Toy Marketing Machine. And that Bluefish Saltwater Special
may scare every trout out of the run.

But we like the sense of adventure and expansive spirit that comes
with offbeat angling. That and the fact that for every dry hole we
stumble onto or technique that flails, we find one that delights us with
a gusher of fish or a new way to catch them. But we also wonder why
more people aren't more willing to venture down the offbeat path.

Perhaps it has to do with man generally being a sociable creature, filled with desire to conform, is not about to change his basic nature once a fishing rod is thrust in his hands. That nature results in wall-to-wall fishermen along certain stretches of water, with many fishing the same way with similar technique. Think nymphers floating the 8-mile stretch below Yellowtail Dam on the Bighorn River. Think spinner-baiters on Toledo Bend in the latest Ranger Bass Boats. Think dry fly men in tweeds on the Itchen in England. Deviating from the mean in any significant way in these places will result in an anti-social vibe from one's fellow fishers intense enough to make one feel like a complete pariah. In some cases, such deviation is not even allowed under either the public or private rules that govern that water!

Of course, conventional wisdom might say that people are clumped together fishing in one spot using mostly one technique because that spot is where the fish are, and that technique is the one that catches them. There is obviously some truth to such conventional wisdom—otherwise, it wouldn't be called that.

Then again, along that crowded section of water where everyone is fishing the same way, there may be one or two people who wonder if something different is worth trying. Maybe they are bored of doing the same thing in the same place as everyone else and catching the same fish. Maybe they believe that there might be better ways and places to catch fish. Or maybe they are just tired of hearing the same dirty jokes and stale fish stories told for the umpteenth time. Whatever the reason, they break the bonds of social convention, damn its consequences, and set down a different path. Whether they will be successful or not is unknown. The point is in the trying, as all those famous mountaineers like to say.

Then lo-and-behold after one or two folks break away down the off-beat path and report back, then a few more follow. Then more come in the spirit of manifest destiny, particularly if the predecessors experience some success. Before you know, conventional wisdom has been modified to embrace what was previously thought of as unacceptable. And a bunch of fishermen are now fishing in a new way and in a new place.

When thinking of concepts that once were considered offbeat but have now been accepted into the ranks of angling normalcy, two immediately come to mind: belly boats (or float tubes as their manufacturers prefer to say) and the Clouser minnow.

I don't know who invented the belly boat. A brilliant person without a doubt. This individual was undoubtedly confronted with a fishy area that was too small to allow access by a boat or canoe yet too deep to wade. Stealth was also needed. Perhaps the innovator—harkening back to days as a lazy youth drifting down the river, a cooler of

Rheingold Extra Dry tethered to
his float–tried to fish using a
truck inner tube but got frustrated over the difficulty of casting
while staying propped up inside
the tube. Then maybe while
playing in the family pool with
his kids, he reached for one of
their little seahorse floaties and a
flash of inspiration burst forth,
resulting in a marriage of the
tube with the seat-in concept of
the floaty. Undoubtedly, the first
few forays in those initial designs
onto public water were greeted

with derision by boaters and bankers (both those of the fishing and
money lending varieties) alike, not to mention the odd tipping or two.
But after he started catching fish... Now, on many western rivers you
can count as many belly boaters as there are waders.

The story of Bob Clouser is better known. As an unemployed meat
cutter in the early 1980s in hardscrabble Pennsylvania, he had started a
part-time guiding business for smallmouths on the Susquehanna. At the
time, he wondered if a fly could be developed employing the up and
down swimming motion of a jig. He managed to convince the manager
of a nearby manufacturing plant to mill some small, weighted eyes in
the mold of a miniature dumbell, which Clouser proceeded to tie to
the underside of a hook for weedlessness and dress sparsely with buck-
tail. At first, and even to this day by some hidebound traditionalists,
Clouser's invention was looked down upon by the fly fishing elite as a
mere spinning lure attached to a fly line. But after he started catching
fish.... Now, on my home waters of the Chesapeake Bay, it is downright unconventional to fly fish for blues or stripers with anything but a
Clouser minnow.

In chronicling our offbeat pursuits in this book, particularly if it
achieves some level of success, there is always a fear that the masses
will take note and apply. Once everyone takes up offbeat angling then,
by its very nature, it can no longer be called offbeat angling. Besides,
casting mulberry flies to inner-city carp just isn't the same when there
are dozens standing next to you and doing the same. Ditto for dodging bulldozers in pursuit of quarry bass.

An even worse thought would be if some creature of pop culture
success (or rather excess) were to adopt our creed in a mass market
kind of way. Picture a certain rap star whose name is synonymous with

candy that melts in your mouth, not in your hand. He has decided to produce an "alternative" album (a la Bruce Springsteen) to complement his traditional streetrap fare. He struts on the cover, wagging in your face a neoprene-covered glove with the fingertips cut off, his bloodshot eyes peering over the tops of a pair of Action Optics's best polarized lenses. His baggy waders barely hanging onto his hips and an L.L. Bean multi-pocketed fishing vest hanging loosely on a bare torso. The album, *Throwin' Da Loop Da Loop*, achieves both popular and critical acclaim and the song, "Girl, You May Be Fly, But Don't Be Touchin' My Rod," makes it to #1 on the charts. Even the goody-too-shoes types who frequently condemn rap for its violent and sexual content praise the album for its focus on outdoor themes and its encouragement of America's youth to take up one of our most traditional pastimes.

Subsequent to the album's success imagine, if you will, the following conversation between two distinguished members of the prestigious Fly Fishing Order of the Coif, Sir Chalmers Castworthy and Godfrey Lightibbets, Esq.:

Castworthy: Hello there, Lightibbets. Looking forward to the spring trip on the Letort, are we?

Lightibbets: I'm afraid it's not in the cards this year, Sir Chalmers.

Castworthy: Why not? Trying to fool those wise old browns becoming just a bit too frustrating?

Lightibbets: No, it's not that. I've been wanting to try this offbeat angling.

Castworthy: Hmm?

Lightibbets: It's something my son Godfrey has gotten me into. He says it's getting popular because of this music star, M and N.

Castworthy: What exactly is this offbeat angling? I can't say I've heard of M and N either.

Lightibbets: Well, for example, there is this aquamarine-looking lake that you see just off the New Jersey Turnpike, right where all those chemical plants are. It's probably on a Superfund site, but it looks like it might hold bass and Goddy and I bet that no one ever fishes it. He says it's a place a brown water boy would love.

Castworthy: Lightibbets! You are passing up the clear, spring waters of the Letort to fish some smelly Superfund site? And in New Jersey of all places?

Lightibbets: It's close by and we might even bring our spinning gear....

Quite frankly, Chris and I don't expect rap stars, members of the Fly Fishing Order of the Coif, or the masses to take up offbeat angling. The social order will hold in fishing as it does elsewhere. There just won't be that many volunteers when Chris decides on an impromptu stocking of the municipal water fountain at one of those bucolic Connecticut hamlets near where he lives. Nor do I expect to compete for bank space down at the pond by the Vietnam Veterans Memorial, with the exception of making room for the tour bus group from Bucyrus, Ohio who stop to feed the ducks, or for Tractor Man if he decides to park his tractor in another protest against U.S. tobacco policy.

If a few more adopt the offbeat angling creed, as a result of this book or for any other reason, that's O.K. There is always the next boulder to scale over, another overlooked, goop-filled pond under an overpass, and a new saltwater special to try in that trout-filled run.

Fish Dude with a 'Tude

Fantasy Island

By Christopher Arelt

The sudden play of light caught his eye. A visitor approaching? No one had been announced. He craned his neck. On the rug, one, two, three dogs passed out in a heap. Ahah! There, atop the coffee table. The melting ice had shifted in his glass and met the westerly rays of p.m. sun just so, refracting a beam directly onto his face. Now what were the odds of that, he mused. Clearly a cue from on high to make some headway on his gin and tonic. He tightened his stomach muscles, pulled his chest in, squeezed his buttocks, lengthened *and* tightened his leg muscles ("length from strength") and rolled up and out of the couch (with control), arms extended to offer up pen and magazine (a substantially complete Sunday *New York Times Magazine* crossword puzzle in pen trumps a fully-complete pencil version) in exchange for a delicious afternoon cocktail.

"Perry Fontaine was not a great man."

This was a verdict he feared like no other. He suspected, strongly at times, and more and more frequently, that it might be so. And yet if anyone had ever suggested such a thing, himself included (and especially), it would be utterly devastating. A textbook case of midlife crisis? He was forty after all. The daily, weekly, monthly victories—an inked puzzle, a 10 k race, why, he had even been trying his hand at *fly-fishing* of all things in recent months (useful as an ice-breaker)–were proving increasingly futile. The big picture of his life was growing more vivid. Apparent and irrevocable. Etched. He wasn't sure he liked it.

And yet he could easily, and often did, arrange the evidence in what seemed to him a very persuasive, indeed irrefutable, inventory and come up with a description of a man that would have them rising from their seats. College graduate, financially successful and now independently wealthy (admittedly a lot of old money) with homes in Greenwich, Boca Grande, and here on Amity Island. Well-read, very well-liked. A winning smile, a firm handshake. No wife, but a deep list of blue-chip prospects, several of whom would be attending this evening's edition of the renowned Fontaine party series. And on top of all that, what a fine name. Who wouldn't want to be Perry Fontaine?

"I wouldn't," growled the Skipper as he threw the throttle in reverse and eased into the North End Landing Dock. The Skipper was a burly man who resembled his namesake, Alan Hale, Jr., in stature but with a cantankerous personality that formed a generous berth between him and his species. Fifty-five going on eighty, apparently he woke up on the wrong side of the bed *every* morning. Islands and boats provide ideal habitats for recluses and misanthropes, and the Skipper had found safe harbor on Amity Island many years ago. Among his myriad enterprises was a $75 no-frills, half-day, guided fishing adventure that clung tight to the island's varied and abundant shoreline. This morning's guest was Chip "Pig" Frost. When Chip had turned fourteen he liked the age so much he vowed to remain an adolescent indefinitely. Now twenty-eight, he was a full double his behavioral age but not ready to wave the white flag just yet. Among Chip's acquired tastes: Offbeat Angling.

"I don't see what the big deal is," Chip rejoined, excerpts from an anti-no trespassing campaign speech starting to seep into the conversation. "This is a beautiful island, one of 'the last ten great places' according to the Nature Conservancy. These people aren't around 99% of the time anyway and, even if they are, they probably don't venture far from air-conditioning." They had been out in the Skipper's boat, a 24' wide-beam mini Lobsterman, since before dawn, fishing for stripers near jetties in some unusually snotty conditions for early July in New England. It had given way to crisp, blue skies. The Skipper hadn't had much to say other than "nice weak" when Chip somehow managed an 8-pound weakfish. That was a while ago and Chip had been handling the conversation single-handedly ever since. When Skip did speak he didn't look at you, which made you nervous about looking at him. He was staring Chip in the eye as his silence ended.

"Folks from the South Side got houses so big there's rooms they never been in. They got butlers and maids, swimming pools, ocean view, helicopter to off-island. Barely room left for the likes a me. But I ain't gonna fight it, I'm just gonna go fishing in the ocean like everyone else. You're not gonna catch anything near as big as what you already caught this morning. I wouldn't try it and neither should you."

Chip considered that maybe silence was golden, then charted a conciliatory course as they disembarked and began unloading tackle. "You're right, why come out to an island in the ocean to fish freshwater. It doesn't make sense."

The Skipper emitted a primitive sound, presumably Seaman for "Finally he gets it." Helping the youngster with his gear, he felt a rare tinge of fondness. "You get a chance, send me a picture of that 40-pounder. She was yar."

"Sure will. Hey Skip, I'm off to the Mermaid Inn, first round's on the Pig if you'd care to join me."

"Doubtful."

In truth, the Skipper knew the whereabouts of any number of extra-large saltwater Island denizens. He especially enjoyed taking unwitting guests over to "the Frat House," a circular grouping of black rocks that can accommodate a small boat. Once inside, drop a clawless fiddler and the chances were favorable for a photo opportunity with a trophy blackfish. Big fish made for happy guests which meant big tips. The striper Chip had caught was, frankly, a yawner, ever since the big striper comeback of the past decade ("Show me a 60-pounder, then we'll think about getting excited"). The Skip also knew a good deal more than he had let on about the inland ponds his guest was obsessing about. Nowadays, most were on private property, but when he moved here the island had been a very different place. Mainly farms belonging to a handful of hearty year-round souls, with a modest fishing outpost huddled in an inlet on the island's leeward northeast side. Why would anyone venture into this often-difficult and at times brutal environment? As sprawl escalated and the mainland's shore filled in, the island's appeal as a tourist destination took shape. Each year a few more blankets on the beach, another house-turned B&B, a second and then a third fish-house turning a profit.

The Skipper, alias John Williamson, had some twenty years earlier taken up residence in the tiny cluster of fisherman's cottages, fishing as a deck hand and filling in with odd jobs in down times. During the shoulder seasons he traversed most of the 8x12-mile island on foot and over the years had developed a thorough knowledge of the landscape. This included the location, size and depth of the numerous ponds that dotted the place. Because the island was formed of clay, it had literally hundreds of naturally-occurring basins that held water year-round. And, it turned out, some very hungry largemouth bass that had been stocked there experimentally by the state in the '50s. The tranquility of such a pristine oasis had a special appeal and, somewhat ironically, John Williamson found the ultimate antidote for civilization inland, not at sea. A morning spent on one of these ponds was bliss, ocean mist rolling across, the occasional scavenger bird paying a visit, the bees buzzing atop the lily pads. Then the silence broken by a hulking large-mouth launching free of the water to engulf a cleverly-presented frog-bait dropping off a pad. Pure heaven. Over time, the memories them-selves proved powerful enough to satisfy.

The Mermaid Inn was hopping as usual for a Saturday afternoon in July. The vintage scene included scantily-clad beach babes, buff beach hunks, and a sprinkling of salts getting hammered early and liking it. Chip was parked near the end of the bar, facetiously named "Mahogany Shoals."

"Thought I'd buy you that pint you promised me."

"Old-timer!" Immediately Chip wasn't sure about the political cor-rectness of his remark, but there appeared to be no consequence. "Barkeep, a pair of Magic Hats, #9 of course. I didn't think you'd...I'd see you again so soon."

"I'd like to sink a few but I've got 'a penchant for pugnacity,' or so I've been told, when swimmin' in drink. Plus, I've got another charter at dawn. I came by to tell you a few things."

"Fire away." Chip wondered where this was going.

"Those ponds you were goin' on about. I do know them. Very well. Haven't been fishing fresh in a dogfish's age, but I'd like to help you out. Because kid..." He paused and looked Chip in the eye for a second time. Was Skip actually getting soft all of a sudden? "They're a gold mine."

Chip felt all tingly, like a European supermodel had suddenly walked into his bedroom.

"There's one in particular, very private, very difficult to get to. But so full of fish it's worth every scratch. I reckon the state record's in there a few times over." (the state record sat at 10 pounds 6 ounces) Skip then went into detail about the access route, the best spots on the pond, the ideal baits.

"I'm there. Thanks, Captain!"

"I recommend you get outta this place soon. You'll want to be in there at first light."

"Why wait, Old timer, I'm there...now!"

The Skipper smiled for the first time, exposing mirror skylines of yellow-brown structures. Chip downed both beers, offered an enthusiastic thumbs-up, jumped off the barstool and shot out the door. The Skipper watched through the window as he grabbed his rods, threw a pack on his back, hopped on a rented bike and tore off down the street.

"That kid reminds me a somebody."

As the afternoon progressed, Perry Fontaine thought less and less about his lurking uncertainty and more about that evening's festivities. He enjoyed parties immensely, especially his own. Each summer he made a point of giving at least three: Kickoff, Summer Swelter, and "Say it ain't over," an end-of-season affair. In fact, it never *was* over for Perry since he left for Boca Grande in October. But the parties in Amity were his best. Giving top parties was an art form, according to the top magazines. So in a sense Perry was an artist, even though he used a consultant to conceptualize, plan and oversee them and an expanded staff to execute them. He was the producer of the party, and producers were artistic.

Tonight's party was Summer Swelter: Hawaiian theme, including tongue-in-cheek gestures to the trite—tiki torches, staff in grass skirts, a limbo contest. But these would be mixed with authentic Hawaiian fare, including exotic fish flown in fresh from the Big Island, decorative Kuaian flora (also flown in fresh), and an accomplished dance troupe. Dessert was to be a volcano cake. Trite themes became nuanced and acceptable amid the seriously-upscale décor and ambiance of Perry's island retreat. The overall effect, as Janine from Event Exclusives had put it, was "a low-culture patina selectively tainting a firm substrate of high." Striking the correct balance was the key to achieving a favorable rating in the write-ups that followed.

Balance was also critical for the guest list. To a point. Cultural and intellectual diversity, but not economic. Some new faces absolutely, but mostly familiar. Descending generational representation. And of course, 60-40 female, the maximum imperceptible ratio of imbalance—and of that, 10 percent blue chips. All this expertise derived from Perry's extensive empirical investigation, culled from decades of experience and grouped into a body of knowledge termed "Racket Science." It was an oral theory typically expounded through the microphone of a late night/early morning cigar. The goal of all this effort, all these principles, the planning, the headaches, the expense was, of course, sex.

Chip had been born with a compass in his head, a nose for water, and a natural resistance to poison ivy, all of which served him well in his offbeat angling. The Skipper knew the island like the back of his stubby, weatherbeaten hand. Chip had never set foot on it before. But he had gotten wind of the fresh water opportunities from a weekly fishing report on the internet—some vacationing tourist had stumbled onto one not far from his summer rental and proceeded to clean up—with a Clouser Minnow no less.

A rough topographical map, also downloaded from the 'net, was all he had when he stepped off the ferry that weekend. Combined with the Skipper's colorful (if vague) rantings, Chip now felt that he had pinpointed his destination with cartographic exactitude. He headed southwest out of town, on one of only two roads that interconnect Amity. The throngs immediately dissipated and he soon felt he had stepped back in time as he peddled along the bumpy, barely-paved roads that rolled up and down a patchwork of open fields outlined by stone walls supporting huge drifts of *rosa rugosa*. The privet hedge was common here as well, in bloom and smelling fantastic.

The marker Chip was looking for was a kid's lemonade stand, black, with a row of three large yellow lemons painted on the front. Somehow he couldn't visualize the Skip taking note of this, much less actually stopping to buy a Dixie cup from some ten-year-old entrepreneurs. But there it was, and soon after a narrow grassy trail marked by a single stone, just as described. Chip brought his bike down the trail until out of sight of the road, then tossed it into the brush on one side, carrying on with only rod and pack. The trail got progressively narrower and before long he was in thick, prickly brush, the grass below his only remaining guide. He was trailblazing now, but he knew instinctively that he was getting close. He caught bits of shimmer through the branches, and it was slightly soggy under foot. He emerged from the brush—fell out, really—and landed on his butt.

There it was, only an acre or so in size, but a *virgin* acre. No way anyone had been down that trail in years. He noticed that his landing pad was unusually tidy. He shifted his gaze from the pond and over a plane of *sod* to a figure standing not a stone's throw away. Motionless. Regarding him—the interloper. A wave of dread passed through him. "Oh geez, I'm busted already." He considered flight and was about to dive into the brush when he stopped to laugh out loud.

It was a statue.

Life-sized. Marble. A Roman god or some such ancient fellow who was wearing a pelt over one shoulder, a menacing gaze, and little else (one of the Skipper's ancestors perhaps?). Chip moved closer to take a look. As he did, an amazing apparition of a house swam into view, bathed in the evening light. He came full up to the statue and verified that this was indeed a distant focal point. A series of tiers, trees, walls and shrubs cascaded symmetrically toward him. Chip and the statue stood center stage as viewed from the expansive terrace and grouping of

French doors beyond. The house was truly an estate, the stuff of movie sets. From Chip's perspective, the best thing was this: the relationship between house and pond was a dogleg, with the intimidating statue manning the knee. Thus, the pond was not in direct view of the house, and vice versa. So unless someone felt compelled in the fading light to traverse the 200-some odd yards to the far reaches amid a cloud of mosquitoes, gnats and deer ticks for a glimpse of a swampy pond, he was on his own.

The sounds he loved—the hum of insects on the water, the smackings of assorted fish at the surface, and one or two penetrations of the surface by some aggressive types. He felt in his pack for a home-grown plastic worm, scented at the factory and then "ac-scent-uated" in Chip's special sauce. A "crème fatale," in black of course. Slipping this over an offset 2/0 hook he tossed it skyward and felt immediate resistance, strong, a split second after it hit the water.

The evening was off to a fine start. The first guests were arriving now, the hum of the party had begun. A gentle steel drum melody in the background, plenty of bubbly flowing, and a welling chatter.

"Joan, darling, you must tell me who does your pool, I've had filthy luck this year."

"Perry! You old dog, you. What's goin' on? How's it hangin'? Good times, good times. I'm off to snag a dark-and-stormy, catch you later my man."

"Those damned windmills. Okay, great, they're 'eco-friendly,' but they look like something from *2001 A Space Odyssey*. I mean, okay it *is* 2003 but, well, they're...ugly."

"Mr. Fontaine, you must protect me! I don't know a single one of these men except *you!*"

Roger that, my dear.

The chatter drowned out the steel drums as a second wave of guests tumbled in, then a third, and the chatter became a din. The flow of humanity through the front door shot like water from a dike hole, slowing only to acknowledge the host and then coursing toward the infinite granite bar. Eddies of guests formed in front, swirling clusters which swelled and shrank and intermingled and gradually multiplied to fill the space entirely, thereafter spinning off one by one into adjacent spaces to alleviate the pressure. Those spaces would follow suit, crowd, dissolve, and the process would repeat. Perry had seen this phenomenon before, at every party he'd ever given. Amazingly, he could and had predicted when and which cluster would eventually land in the game room this evening, and as he ostensibly "happened" in from the servants' passage he brimmed with self-pride at the accuracy of his forecast.

Wendy Peete, Ty Riggington, Keely Ouvier, Betty Jo Halperstammer. Wendy was a blue chip, Keely and Betty Jo two long-time adoring fans, and Ty was temporarily estranged from his partner Hal. And now, Perry himself. The odds were staggering. A royal flush.

"Boys and girls, are we having a good time?"

"Perry, I've been looking everywhere for you!" Could Betty Jo really be this enthusiastic *all* the time? Perry had never seen her otherwise. "This party is so very. Oh, and I have a prognostication!" She cupped her hands to form a megaphone. "Betty Jo Halperstammer is the winner of tonight's First Annual Limbo Contest...by a nipple!"

Clearly, the girl was already well on her way. There was no value in flouting an inebriate, especially in front of a blue chip. Perry deftly changed course, gesturing to the far wall.

"My collection of vintage fly fishing apparatus!"

It truly was magnificent, or so said the curator of the Catskill Fly Fishing Museum when he flew in special last month to have a look. Perry had opted for authenticity in the game room; these trophies played a big part and were great conversation pieces.

"Here we have a bamboo prototype from the first days of the House

of Hardy, Alnwick, England, circa 1880. Brothers William and John were ahead of their time."

He continued to a glass case set on an angle atop an intricately-carved wood base. "Quill Gordons hand-tied by the Catskill master Theodore Gordon himself." The group drew up close to have a look.

"And this is the 1959 fishing journal of none other than the mighty Ernie Schweibert!" They gazed in bewilderment.

As Perry went on (he was careful never to drone) he kept a furtive eye on Wendy. She seemed impressed, even mesmerized, by the breadth of his knowledge. And the means required to assemble such a collection went without saying. All that remained, he reasoned, was a demonstration of his physical mastery of the sport. Once that had been clearly evidenced, he would appear some kind of demi-god, taking pity on her by agreeing to share a bed later that night.

"The beauty, the art of fly fishing, cannot be described in words. Rather than wax eloquent, you must *see* the fly fisherman in action to fully appreciate the majesty of this purest of communes with nature and her glory."

With that important preamble in place, Perry ushered them back to the main hall that led to the Sun Room, a cavernous space with 12-foot French doors opening onto the rear terrace.

"Perry's going to show us fly fishing!" gushed Keely.

The word drifted around and, as predicted, about half of the guests made their way to the Sun Room. Opposite the French doors had been suspended a monumental projection screen. The screen was blank at this moment and served as a backdrop for Perry as he stepped in front for a few words.

"Thank you for coming. Tonight's theme, as you know, is of another great island. The sea and her bounty offer so much pleasure to islanders the world over, and to inject a bit of education into this evening's event I thought I'd offer some of my expertise on the fine art of fly fishing."

This was met with a rousing show of support.

"Although this sport has enjoyed a tremendous surge in popularity over recent years, especially in terms of its marine applications, few people realize that fly fishing actually had its start in saltwater, and on our themed archipelago no less."

The crowd was abuzz now with enthusiasm and surprise, even admiration. A smile crossed Perry's face. "Hundreds of years ago,

"Kajagoogoo"

the Hawaiian Islands' waters were home to a fish which the people called Kajagoogoo. It was a beautiful fish, yellow with blue marking and a mane of bright yellow threadlike tentacles on its head. The fish were abundant, grew to great size, and were known to taste delicious. However, very few could be caught. These fish were sophisticated and they spooked easily. Nets and hand lines were clumsy and useless. Occasionally a native might have a single strike but these "one-hit wonders" would never strike again. Moreover, although they grew very large, they preferred to feed only on the tiniest of baitfish. The task of getting an attractive bit of food sufficiently isolated proved daunting."

"Then a prominent native realized that by using a heavier line, made from interwoven boar hairs, and attaching it to a bamboo pole, he could use the weight of the line to cast a very light object quite far. The results were immediate and overwhelming. Soon, people were dining on Kajagoogoo for breakfast, lunch and dinner. In fact, the Kajagoogoo is now extinct, it was simply too delicious for its own good."

"That's so sad," Betty Jo could be heard remarking.

"The proud inventor was made the first king of the big island. You may have heard of him, Chief Boba Phet."

The crowd, which had now grown to include nearly all in attendance, murmured. A few nodded assuringly.

"Today, as mentioned earlier, fly fishing is enjoying unprecedented popularity, although many of the finer points–matching the hatch, casting and presentation–remain elusive to most."

At this point the talk had so captivated the audience that a question-and-answer period seemed in order. This was something Perry wasn't sure he had the imaginative stamina to endure. So he cut to the chase. "And now, for your further edification and entertainment, an exclusive remote broadcast, live, from our very own pond, in which I will demonstrate this time-honored practice."

Thunderous applause as Perry left the room. The lights dimmed and the screen lit up with a fancy title block:

"Perry Fontaine–Master Fly Fisherman"
Episode Four
"The Cast"

The guests were positively ecstatic. The blue chips giggled. Betty Jo squealed.

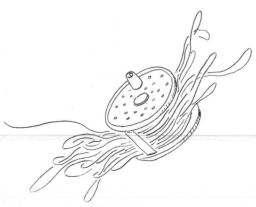

The title lingered, presumably to allow Perry to make his way to the distant pond. Finally, the image cut to a scene of the pond, the fisherman and his rod majestically silhouetted against a brilliant orange sunset.

Chip had just undone a nasty snarl in his reel and removed a generous clump of hydrilla weed which had accumulated on his dragonfly during the downtime. He had no idea of the timeliness. Having reeled in completely to resolve the ordeal, he now set about loosing line just as a tiny red light appeared in a nearby conifer.

"What a cast!" he remarked as the fly alighted in a tasty-looking crevice in the pads. Somewhere in the distance he swore he heard a chorus offer their congratulations.

In the game room, Perry turned to his friend. "Well, Skipper, what do you think? I mean, nobody writes music or plays instruments any more. Hell, P. Diddy is the richest man on the planet, in fact he just bought the place next door."

"Image is everything. You da man, Perry. You da man."

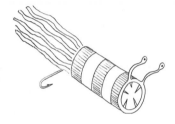

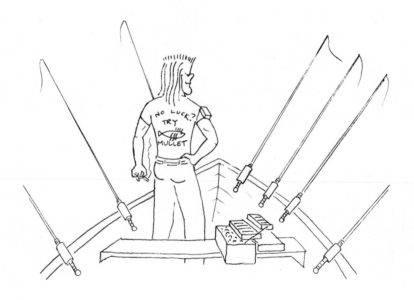

Them Fish Ain't Got No Chance

By Hand

By Sebastian O'Kelly

Long before fast-action fly rods, polymer-coated lines and fluoro-carbon tippets. Long before 5:1 retrieve spinning reels, double-jointed crankbaits, and cooler-sized tackle boxes. Long before nets, traps and trawlers. Long before even hooks and lines, bows and arrows, and spears of the primitive type displayed in ancient cave drawings. Long before there were any other means man has since invented to catch fish.

There were, and there are, hands.

When early man first peered into water and saw a fish, he surely, operating on a combination of instinct and hunger, tried to grab it. No doubt he found his first hairy-pawed efforts to secure dinner unsuccessful, but after a number of tries and perhaps a few Cro-Magnan generations, he learned the stealth, technique and dexterity needed to catch fish with his hands. He also had to overcome fear–fear of drowning, of other critters in the water, and, probably the biggest fear of them all–the fear of the unknown and what the hell could be down there.

The essence of those techniques has been passed from generation to generation, all the way to modern days where in certain parts, despite all those advances in catching technique and technology, man still catches fish with his hands.

Two primary techniques have survived all those years. There have been modifications to be sure–man and fish are adaptable creatures–but

they are otherwise unchanged from when old Cro Mag developed
them. One, familiar to lovers of Shakespearean sonnets and highly
praised by the Good Bard, is called "tickling." It takes place in cool,
clear waters and entails spotting and stalking a fish, most likely a trout,
then crouching along the bank and slowly reaching into the water
under the fish, gently stroking the underside of its belly, putting it into a
state of relaxation. Once the hand is in place, you grab the fish and flip
it up onto the bank in one motion.

I tried tickling a few times as a kid. I didn't have the patience or skill.
Besides, catching fish on a rod and reel was more fun and enough of a
challenge. I did catch a trout once by hand, a leftover from the stocking
truck that survived the opening month's assault. It was finning itself in
the open (made sluggish by the summer sun in a warm water river it
probably never should have been stocked in in the first place) and an
easy catch for an 11-year-old with good hands from fielding Little

League grounders. I admired the fish for a few moments then put him back in the river, taking some time to revive him. Thinking back, I doubt he lived out the week before high water temps or a predator claimed him.

From the offbeat perspective, it is the second technique, called "noodling," or grabbling in a few places, that is far more interesting. It is a technique practiced by men (and perhaps the very tough and very rare woman) with monosyllabic first names, gun racks in their pickups, tattoos across their chests, men who live hard lives and earn their ways with their hands–pipefitters, oil drillers, power linemen. These men are not part of the fly fishing set. Sir Chalmers Castworthy and Godfrey Lightibbets would never associate with them, except when the plumbing needed fixing.

But probably what distinguishes and unites them to a man are shredded skin, hardened scabs, and even permanent scars spider webbed across their bare forearms. They are the badge of the noodler, the hunter of big, dark fish hidden in the shallow lakes, slow rivers, fetid backwaters and murky oxbows that typify the waters of the Middle South. That and a wild, jumpy look in the eyes that comes to people who spend their time pushing risk. For noodling is about reaching into the unknown in places where you can't sometimes see, probing with bare hands in a most vulnerable way for fish (and God knows what else is down there with them) that are powerful and frightening-looking. It's about that monster lying under your bed waiting to grab you when you were a kid. Only this time instead of taking a running jump into the safety of the covers, you're leaning over the side and reaching underneath, exposed to that unknown thing and owning up to instinctual fear that can't be completely settled with a stiff drink and a trip to the bookstore to get the latest self-help book, or in the kid's case, a soothing hug from Mom or Dad.

The quarry in noodling is a beast Mark Twain, in his works, claimed could carry off small children. He is referring to that bottom-dweller and eater of refuse (and anything else it can get its overly large mouth around) –the catfish. The two biggest species and the ones of most interest for noodling are the blue and flathead. Twain-style child abduction is something of an exaggeration of what these beasts are capable, but in a land-based reversal, the biggest of these two cats, both of which can exceed 100 pounds, could suck down a small dog paddling in the open water like a Texas roughneck downing a Bud.

The basic technique is pretty straightforward. Find a hole or hidey spot where a big catfish is laying. Spring is the best time as that's when they move into the shallows to spawn, seeking depressions in the bottom, holes underneath big tree stumps or the opening of a 55-gallon drum planted by a noodler seeking a leg up. Once you find the cat, reach down with your hand toward his head. If he's feeling passive, run your fingers under his belly to further soothe him. For some reason, that stroking causes an opening of the mouth (if he's in an aggressive mood you can skip this step as you will become very much aware of his presence as soon as your hand gets anywhere near his mouth). Now is the moment of truth. Thrust your hand as far down his throat as possible and to the side where you can grab the side of his gill plate, the idea being to pull him out of the hole and up onto a boat or bank before he can do too much damage to your arm. Then hold on because all hell is gonna break loose!

Catfish don't have teeth per se, but rather a series of sandpaper-like bumps which are used to hold their prey before swallowing it whole. Anyone who has ever caught a catfish on rod and reel knows that two favored fighting techniques of cats are the head shake and the 360 degree body twist. That is no different with noodling. Imagine a couple of belt sanders working a circle around your forearm with vise-like pressure. Catfish also have non-retractable spines the size of 4-inch nails. While they thrash around the chance of getting punctured by a spine...well, it is certainly higher than winning the lottery and not near as joyous an occasion.

There are variations on the technique. Some like to reach down into a hole blindly with no gloves, operating strictly by feel, clearly the most pure and hardcore approach. Others use gloves and a mask. That way you have some protection and you can presumably see (though these tend to be pretty murky waters) what you are about to stick your hand into. Having a buddy along is good safety advice, if only to help you win the tug of war with an especially big cat. A 60-pounder is considered a big fish by noodling standards. I've never heard of a 100-pound fish being caught. Maybe because at that size it is the noodler who ends up being the one caught. There are rumors of men who have gone noodling and never returned. But that could always be an excuse for skipping out on the wife and heading for parts unknown.

There are other critters besides catfish who live in these holes. Water moccasins may be present. The thought of one sinking its poisonous fangs into your thumb is not comforting. But it pales when considering hand-to-mouth combat with an alligator snapper. The alligator snapper is a larger, steroid-enhanced relation of the better known common snapping turtle. It frequents many of the same Southern waters as blues and flatheads and likes to be in the same types of hiding spots from which it can ambush its prey, which is typically fish of about the size and shape of your hand. If you put your hand in the mouth of an alligator snapper, you may well get it back but there is a good chance you won't be flipping the bird with it ever again, or wearing a wedding ring either.

That's why some noodlers like to prospect potential spots with a stick first. If they feel something soft and moving, then it's likely a cat. If it's hard and moving, then it's probably a turtle and possibly an alligator snapper.

If the stick comes back snapped in half, then it's definitely the latter and time to get out of there.

Every few years a national publication, typically with a literary bent, will run a story about noodling. Recently, a film documentary, *Okie Noodling*, was completed by an indie film maker. The tone of these pieces ranges from a down–the-nose, "look what these crazy, dumb rednecks are doing now" to a more charitable Charles Kuraltish take celebrating noodling as a unique part of cultural and regional Americana.

I take the latter view, though I've never gone noodling. I could offer up all kinds of excuses—work and family responsibilities; not knowing anyone to show me the ropes; and not being from that part of the country. But they are all excuses of convenience. I know deep within still lies that fear of what's under the bed, that fear of the unknown and frightening critters imprinted into the human genetic code.

So I imagine a trip instead. Chris and I fly to an airport in Texas that only a Southwest or Jet Blue would arrange service for. Then it's a 3-hour drive to Whiskerton on the Tex-Arkana border to noodle in the local hotspot, Lake Mudcat. There's not much in Whiskerton. It is a place where it's O.K. to ride dirt bikes and ATVs on the streets and folks treat the town's only stoplight more like a stop sign. We stop at a quickie mart for directions and to load up on some Cokes and beef jerky.

We arrive at Lake Mudcat. It's shallow and brown as a latte—perfect large cat water. Chris pulls a mask and fins from his bag. He is the frog-man today, the proverbial rod, line and bait while I supervise and assist from above the waterline. I inspect the mask. It is encrusted with mold from too long a stay in the dank basement, a forgotten cast off until now from childhood days snorkeling in the Long Island surf.

"Has it been disinfected? Is it up to the task?" I ask, holding the mask at arm's length.

"Assuredly so." He snatches it from me and puts it on. It is a dubious fit at best but it is he not I who will have to negotiate face-to-face with the bottom-feeder. We wade out carefully, probing for depressions in the bottom with our feet. Chris stops.

"I think I just felt one." I sidle over. Chris starts huffing and puffing for what could be a long time underwater. He submerges, my hands on his shoulders for stabilization. 10, 20, 30 seconds go by, the water still. My heart pounds, waiting for the underwater explosion, that quiet moment evidenced in all shark movies before the big attack.

Suddenly, the water churns, bodies writhe—Chris is awrassling with a big'un! My legs are taking more hits than an NFL lineman on a Sunday afternoon. Something sizable slides past. I do the Arkansas hot foot—no way am I going to get prickered by an angry cat. Then everything goes quiet. I carefully probe the water with my hands. I can't see past two inches in. I shuffle my feet hoping to bump into a body. No Chris. I shout his name. I have a very ominous feeling. Has he met his match with the Hades of the Deep?

There is a commotion behind me. Chris is scrambling up the bank. He does a jig, his flippered feet flapping to the side like some giant goonybird. Curses spill from his mouth. He is holding up a de-digitized hand while he hops about.

It has taken 30 years, but the turtles finally have their revenge and have gotten their man! It's finger food tonight, boys!

Maybe one day I'll tackle my fear of this unusual sport. When I do, I'll pack a light bag, leave behind the latest gear and equipment, go noodling and find a link to my ancient forebears. Until then, I'll experience its thrill vicariously and be happy to have enough fingers to write about it.

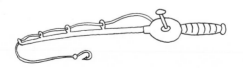

The Spillway

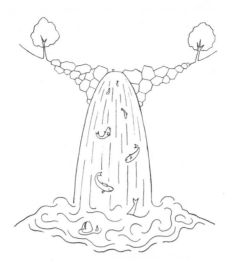

By Christopher Arelt

Winter really wore out its welcome this time around. Mountains of snow that lingered for months. Polar-thick ice that kept skaters happy and fish pressed to the bottom. Even the Connecticut River had frozen solid; adventurous souls were crossing it on foot for the first time in decades. April brought torrential rains and, from the north, a tsunami of a thaw. It seemed as though the ground might never dry out.

The harsh weather created ample opportunity for fly-tying and weight gain. By mid-May Seb and I were itching to lose some flies and a few pounds. A kick-start for both was the impending rite of spring, our Memorial Day pilgrimage to upstate New York. Established during college, it soon became an annual highlight. Ulster County boasts water in all shapes and sizes: slow-moving smallmouth rivers; deep, cold runs like the Esopus; and a host of other ponds, lakes and streams offering endless variety. The granddaddy of them all is the Ashokan Reservoir, former residence of the state record brown trout and current home to aspiring rainbows, browns and walleye; the kind of place where the bait itself can put a healthy bend in your rod.

Despite its prodigious inhabitants, the Ashokan is not our kind of fishing. It's too mainstream and too big and vague, the blue water version of freshwater fishing. Don't get me wrong, we tried it, and on more than one occasion. The promise of a monster trout can have that effect on you. But bobbing around in the chop all day with nary a nibble leaves a distinctly salty taste, and we had passed on it altogether in recent years.

Today we were driving over there out of sheer curiosity. The reservoir is formed and retained by a long, concave dam along the south side. The foul weather had subsided several weeks ago, but we had gotten to thinking. The rivers swell, the ponds spill out on all sides. At the Ashokan, the dam is naturally lower than the surrounding banks. Where exactly does the concentrated overage go? If ever there was a time to investigate, this soggy spring was it. A gazillion gallons must have poured over.

We pulled up alongside the dam, which doubles as a bridge in the manner of the much larger Hoover Dam. There's a lower tier that serves as an ideal platform for bait plunkers, and they reportedly do quite well there, thanks to the general drift of detritus in that direction. This observation played a part in our thinking as well. The concentration of food, an off-season for fish to get reacquainted with the plunkerless damside eatery, and then...Whammo! Massive hydronic forces sending tremendous volume over the edge to who knows where. In the heat of the fray, could some of the diners have gone for a ride as well? We'd soon find out.

It was clear and sunny but, as predicted, big water was still pouring over a depressed segment of the dam. It traveled under the road and, as we crossed to the far side to discover, crashed into a narrow ravine littered with boulders. The water coursed powerfully through the ravine, too fast to fish and probably beyond a fish's ability to hold a position. As we made our way down the incline to a better vantage point, the roar at the dam faded and we detected another, distant one. We scrambled over the boulders and ledge before stopping abruptly at the rim of a cliff. Looking down, we saw for the first time where all this madness was headed.

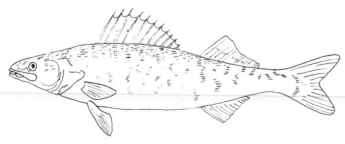

Walleye

A magnificent waterfall, roughly three stories in height, emptied headlong into an immaculate, sky-blue pool. We had our answer to the mystery of the missing reservoir contents. A hidden treasure, made even more attractive by the determination that, without rock climbing apparatus, access from this point was impossible, even for us. Undaunted, we surveyed the pool's circular perimeter and made our way back to the car. It was too chilly for a re-creation of the famous getaway scene from Butch Cassidy, but we would reach this oasis one way or another. Seb recalled passing a fire road en route to the dam and we suspected a connection to our latest find. A clump of pricker bushes near the entrance was identified as an ideal offbeat parking spot. We rammed the old station wagon deep inside and gathered our gear.

The trip down the fire road was long and in those days we brought everything we had, just in case. Tackle boxes, lunches, bait buckets, rods, jackets. Soon we would get a lesson in why it isn't always best to be so prepared. The distant thunder of the falls was barely audible and served as our only guide as the road dissolved into a maze of trails. Eventually we saw the pool through the trees and shortly thereafter emerged near the edge of some unstable, cutaway earth. Below lay an

escarpment of grey stone that resembled the terrain surrounding high-way overpasses. Twenty minutes later we had navigated through a jungle gym of exposed roots and reached the top of the escarpment. The path from here was clear, and it was now or never. We stepped forward and into a free-fall over the remaining distance.

There was some consolation in the fact that no one was watching this scene unfold. The bruises on our egos might have equalled those forming on our bodies. We were still young, at least in our minds, but we'd never pass for a couple of kids out on a lark. Nevertheless, to this day the event stands as a poignant example of the mettle of an offbeat angler. The courage, or rather the valor, to employ a term befitting two such intrepid crusaders. Nothing could turn us from our quest, not the risk of maiming, even the possibility of death. The few. The proud. The Brown Water Boys.

Or, perhaps, the Fools. I'll grant you, it's a fine line. My shin had caught in a nest of brambles on the trip down and was bleeding profusely. Seb sat at the base of the slope and simultaneously rubbed both elbows. One end of his rod rested on his shoulder while the other pointed up-slope to what used to be his tackle box. It had exploded midflight. I felt pangs of guilt, and hunger, as I looked at the sandwiches his mom had packed, coated with dirt and greeting the first of the insect arrivals.

The chaos was rearranged while the pain dulled, soothed by the growing awareness of where our sacrifices had brought us. The mighty Ashokan, famous and popular with fishermen throughout the region, lay close by. But this new discovery was worlds away, we might just as well have landed a pontoon plane on a remote lake in the Canadian wilderness. I looked around for signs of life, or death. No skeletal remains from a tumble gone bad. No bottles, cans or wrappers. And best of all, no tumbleweeds of monofilament rolling in the breeze. The only competition here would be with fish. If indeed they had gone over the dam, their journey to this place would have been as brutal as ours, a one-way rollercoaster ride to whitewater-wash away all memory of Man and his hooks. And now, our punch-drunk prey sat in a glassy pool surrounded by cliffs and barren slopes. Not much food, no choice but to remain patient and hope for the best. If our theory had any merit, there could be some big, dumb, hungry fish in here.

Fishing during the next few hours was a transcendent experience, forever elevating the Spillway to mythic status. The heavy rains had delivered the biggest trout of our angling lives. Seb was the first to succeed, a pesky brown from an eddy near the falls. I followed suit, winning the battle with a smallmouth from atop a solitary boulder by the opposite shore. Each fish was bigger than the last and the expectations rose. A three-pound brown became downright ordinary when there was an eight-pound rainbow following it in. We caught no walleye though, and eventually concluded that they avoided the environs of the dam and thereby the consequent journey. But who could complain after a decade of action in a single day's outing? We squeezed the final casts into the last hint of twilight and felt our way back to the car. The parking ticket on the windshield roughly equalled a pair of one-day, out-of-state fishing permits.

Each year, the constraints of work and adult life make our spring fling a little more complicated and, after all, no time's a bad one. Fact is, there's fantastic fishing year-round in the aquatic wonderland of Ulster County. But when the snow's piled high and the rain won't let up, our thoughts return to the Spillway. We wake in the middle of the night shouting, "They're going over!" and the next morning we're rearranging our schedules to take advantage of a sure thing.

Joey Bag-a-donuts meets Charlie the Tuna

Monkey Fishing

AHOY PRI-MATEY

By Sebastian O'Kelly

When you travel down the offbeat fishing path, coming across the unusual can become common-place; experiencing the extreme not so out-of-the-ordinary; and even seeing the bizarre a some-time thing. But every now and then you come across an activity so outrageous, so off-the-charts, so unbelievable, that it gives pause, if not outright shock and indignation, to even the most non-conformist angler. Such is the case with monkey fishing.

Monkeys are within the primate family and, as such, are the most like humans of all the animal species and also our evolutionary predecessors. If you believe in Creationism, I'm not going to argue with you here, but either way most agree that primates exhibit many human characteristics –love, anger, friendship, jealousy, etc.–and express those characteristics in the most human ways. As a result, we have all sorts of groups and laws protecting them in ways not extended to critters less cuddly. And the general public places them in that category of charismatic mega-fauna, along with grizzlies, lions, dolphins and wolves, that gets them star billing on those animal shows on cable TV; Hollywood starlets embracing their preservation; and exalted status in the pantheon of Disney kids movies. Hurting these animals is akin to burning a flag at the local VFW.

Try telling this to a group of fishermen in the Florida Keys looking for some excitement. Maybe these fishermen have caught more than a few of the Michael Jordan of gamefish, the Silver King himself, that part-time Keys resident otherwise known as the tarpon. The tarpon high, the adrenaline rush so intense, the crack cocaine of fishing, that it drives them to look for something even more intense to maintain that high, something that most people and fishermen would never dare to try or even think of. So when a pharmaceutical company was looking for a place to keep some spare Rhesus monkeys, normally used for drug testing, on a quiet island somewhere, no one had any idea what those poor monkeys might fall prey to.

The monkeys were stashed in the mid-1990s on Lois Key, one of the smaller islands in the Keys. Anytime a boater came near the island, the monkeys would raise an angry chatter, perhaps in anguish at their captivity. In short order, they stripped the place clean of all greenery. The waters near the island were colored brown with feces. The Rhesus were not exactly good environmental stewards.

Then one day, a fisherman or maybe a group of fishermen, no one knows who actually started it, decided to have a little sport with the simians. A heavy saltwater spinning rod was baited with a piece of fruit, which was then lobbed into the trees or mangroves along the shoreline. When a monkey picked up the fruit, the hook was set and the fight was on!

After awhile, the fishermen learned a few things. Kiwis were a favored bait, but were soft and often came off the hook. Monkeys liked apples and oranges a little less but they stayed on the hook better. The fishermen discovered that bringing a hooked, very angry, semi-drowned monkey all the way to your boat was not a good idea. Rhesuses are not huge, an adult weighs about 30-pounds or so, but they can do some serious damage inside the small skiffs that fishermen in these parts like to use. Rods can get broken, tackle boxes flipped over, faces scratched and forearms bitten. So the idea became to set the hook, yank the monkey out of the tree so it hit the water with a big splash, and drag it just long enough so the monkey knows who's boss, then cut the line before it got anywhere near the boat. Call it long distance catch and release.

They say the most fun part was watching the monkey do an impromptu front Gainer into the soiled water. If the tide was running hard, they called it a Monkey Chocolate Swirly. I don't know if the fishermen used barbless hooks. The sport is cruel enough as it is without having some poor monkey howling in pain trying to remove a barbed hook from its palm.

After awhile, the monkeys learned a few things too, namely "monkey see, monkey don't." Any fruit mysteriously found on the island was left alone, or closely inspected before being picked up. A few of the more bold monkeys learned how to steal the fruit without getting hooked, all the while taunting the fishermen out in the boats with loud monkey chatter. Monkey fishing finally came to end when the company removed all the animals from Lois Key in 1999 in response to environmental complaints.

Actually, none of this story is true. It's an urban (or rather an island) myth. Monkey fishing never occurred in the Florida Keys. You might have already figured this out. The cruelty element aside, what sane fisherman, after years of unintended, wayward casts into branches and overbrush and hundreds of dollars of lost tackle as a result, would willingly cast into the trees, no matter what the quarry?

But when writer Jay Forman approached the editors of *Slate Magazine* in 2001 with a story about the subject, they fell for it, hook, line and sinker and ran the piece. After questions about the story's veracity were raised by the *New York Times*, who had been told by area residents and fishermen that no such fishing ever existed, *Slate* editor-in-chief Michael Kinsley issued a mealy-mouthed apology, stating that while there were at one time monkeys on the island and that Forman had actually chartered a fishing boat to catch one, albeit unsuccessfully, the other key elements of the story had been fabricated.

I guess if there is a moral to the story, it is that the old saw holds true. Fishermen like to tell tall tales. And there is always someone gullible enough around to believe them.

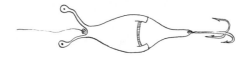

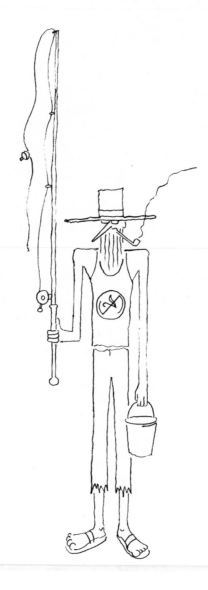

Dry-Fly Purist – NOT

Tamiami Vices

By Christopher Arelt

Getting up early is part and parcel of a fishing life. Even if lunch was a fish's favorite meal, we'd get going before dawn just to gear up. It's more about the suffering. Nothing worthwhile comes without some. At 5 a.m. I pulled into the local convenience store near my point of departure, midway between New York and Boston, to procure a java grande.

"Large coffee, will that be all?"

"Yes, thank you."

"Where you driving this fine morning?"

"Miami."

"Have a nice day."

Surely there was to be some great reward for spanning the entire Eastern Seaboard to do a little offbeat fishing in the citrus state, despite the cashier's insouciance. "The fish you take is equal to the pain you make." Maybe I shouldn't have even gotten coffee, that might cost me a few points. Nothing a twenty-plus hour trip couldn't overshadow.

My stated rationale for driving came to this: short on cash, long on time. Hate waiting around in airports. Hate making choices about what to bring. Hate bringing rods on airplanes. Car rental clerks. Throw in lazy, disorganized, prone to procrastination and here I was, encountering traffic in New Haven. In the back of my SUV was an abstract sculpture of sports equipment, fishing tackle, maps, clothes and fruit.

Road trips always started out with high ideals about eating healthy. I planned on consuming exclusively grapefruits to keep the metabolism going. This would last, it turned out, until I got south of the Mason-Dixon line, where the grapefruits would transform into sweet tea, biscuits and cajun chicken.

Sebastian and I had decided some months earlier that a joint trip was in order. Typically such ventures took place at a mutually-convenient site and in years past we met at his family's home in upstate New York to fish the waters of his youth. Over time we concentrated more and more on a Hudson River tributary that featured legendary smallmouth fishing. Something a bit more exotic seemed in order now, and Seb had discovered in his Internet travels an interesting freshwater phenomenon in Florida: berry fishing for grass carp.

Grass Carp

Berry fishing for grass carp. I thought back to pretend-fishing in my backyard as a kid, the lawn was water and I would practice casting, seeing how close I could come to the edge of Rhododendron Island where the big ones were. As I learned more I became intrigued, but suspicious. Some sun-baked fool called the Land Captain actually sponsored trips for these lumbering creatures in the canals around the country's southernmost tip. Again an image: a gondolier poling gullible sportsmen past rows of pastel hotels, casting to the salsa beat in fetid swill. There were apparently gar present as well. I had caught a gar once, and once was enough. Had experience with guides too. In every case the conversation had included the line, "They were jumping in the

Longnose Gar

boat here last week." Still, this seemed like an ideal addition to our off-beat repertoire. Unusual location. Inscrutable methods. Pariah fish. It had it all. The trip was long, perhaps the tales would be tall.

I switched on Imus only to discover even he wasn't up yet. Definitely too early to be alive. The plan was to meet Seb in D.C. by early afternoon and possibly try a little shad fishing in the Potomac before the big push. He had been raving about it, bombarding me each week with photos displaying a range of attire and grinning expressions beside what appeared to be the same fish. Actually, Seb gets to do a great deal of fishing, or rather makes a point of it, and he is to be commended for his dedication to our sport. In the time we've fished together, his fishing world has expanded while mine has remained provincial. But that is my nature, to find things I like, simple as they may be, and enjoy them to the fullest.

I arrived in D.C. in mid-afternoon, convinced that I didn't want to fish for shad. Seb's photos made me feel as though I had already caught my limit, plus I knew that the ride ahead was going to be brutal. Every minute spent on the Potomac was lost to progress, and it's important to focus on the matter at hand. Teasing big minnows was a trip in itself and for another time. We loaded in his gear, took a few minutes to get reacquainted and shot out of the city before rush hour took hold.

I wouldn't say that I drive recklessly, but I drive fast. No matter how much dawdling precedes the departure, once I'm behind the wheel I'm on a mission to get to point B as quickly as possible. Come midnight we were in South Carolina and settled in at the cheapest among a cluster of roadside motels. By midday next we were well into Florida and Seb was busily scanning the roadsides.

"That looks pretty fishy, maybe we should stop."

"There's chain-link around the entire thing and impenetrable vegetation."

This went on for literally hundreds of miles as we sped south. A trip down the interstate stopping at each one of these prospects seemed like a distinct possibility for a future installment. It would probably take a few weeks to pull it off but, even if it turned out that one out of ten of those fishy-looking puddles held something, it would be worth it.

At mealtime we stopped at a '50s-retro hamburger chain and noticed an oily depression across the parking lot, next to Taco Bell. The debate resumed.

"There could be fish in there. It's got a fountain so the water's circulating."

"The shore is lined with brown foam. Some of it's orange."

"What about over there by that pump, there are some lily pads."

"The shopping cart affords some good structure. Okay, we'll give it a try."

We finished our meal and broke out the rods. Just the image of Seb double-hauling against the backdrop of a fast-food restaurant was worth the delay. "It's a big one, it's huge!" "Excuse me, sir, did you say you want to biggie-size your order?" "That wasn't me, lady, there's some lunatic fishing next to my car."

The Taco Pond was empty, although it was midday so one can't be absolutely certain. As we approached our exit in Fort Lauderdale, we noticed one last highway haven and made a mental note of its where-abouts. Following check-in at our motel we decided to use the remaining light to investigate. Getting to these places is easier said than done. From the highway, they appear to be "right there." That's if you veer off the road and drive through the fence. When you actually exit and make your way back like a sane person it becomes another matter. We navigated through a number of on-ramps, off-ramps, one-ways, parking lots that seemed to connect but didn't, and finally got a visual. There was an empty commuter lot directly across from the pond, separated by only an on-ramp. The pond had a fence around most of it, but not on the highway side. Apparently the D.O.T. had concluded that no one would actually go to the trouble of walking across the on-ramp, up to the highway, around the fence and back to the water. A trifling detour to an offbeat angler. But to a softshell turtle, a major obstacle!

We noticed one pressed up against the chain-link. Poor fellow was headed for the pond and he wasn't going to make it anytime soon. I'd never seen a softshell turtle before so I spent a few minutes examining him. Once I had determined that he was incapable of moving beyond time-lapse photography speed, I picked him up and carried him around. A good deed I trusted the fish gods had noted from above.

Inside the confines of the fence things got pretty nasty. The banks were steep and soggy, there was dense growth armed with thorns and spiny burrs. Our first intimate encounter with Florida's flora. My shoe of choice when fishing is a pair of athletic sandals. These allow for wading in mud and water and, because they have all manner of buckled and velcro straps, they don't get sucked off one's foot when emerging from a sinkhole. In this foreign land, though, I felt a little naked. Who knew what the flora could do, or what might be hiding in it. I treaded lightly toward an opening, a concrete retaining wall with a rainwater outfall. Seb made his way in the opposing direction, an unspoken ritual that allows us to test a new environment most efficiently.

Atop the retaining wall I met the fire ants, who confirmed my footwear concerns. I had a sudden, vague recollection of a warning from my sister in central Florida as I sensed a colony of something making its way onto my feet and ankles. Then all at once the signal was given: "Fire!" It hurt only a little at first, but I knew instinctively that this was more than a mosquito. This was the ground artillery. Dancing a little jig beside the outfall, I brushed them off and plucked the stubborn ones from the web of straps as the waves of pain made their way to my brain. I moved to the outer edge of the wall to avoid any further contact with the earth and its bounty.

I had been casting en route with some, but minor, response. Not sure yet what's going on here. My destination looked particularly promising and on my third cast I hooked something larger than I had the right to hope for. There was a big boil and my drag began to wail. Seb took note from across the way. Whatever it was, it had made an impression but was now wallowing sluggishly in the shallows. It could

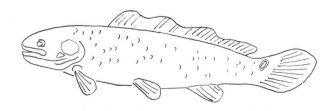

Bowfin

be a sickly bass; the water in here could not promote fitness. I couldn't get down the bank to meet him so I had to opt for the primitive hoist. Just out of the water he snapped off. About two feet long, dark and slender with a long, single dorsal fin and yellow underside. I described him to Seb who, like any shameless angler, had come hustling around to join in the fun. A bowfin, he concluded. Makes a carp look like royalty. Fitting for an environment such as this one. Time to get back to the motel for a hot, sanitizing shower. We recovered from our marathon journey with a marathon "sleep of the dead." Across town, the Land Captain was making ready.

Seb had characterized him after several phone conversations as a salt of the earth type. Sea salt, I would suggest. We met Steve Kantner, alias the Land Captain, outside his apartment building at a humane hour, following an English breakfast. He stood a sturdy six feet, had wavy brown hair and sported a deep, indelible tan. Jeans, a button-down short-sleeved shirt, and a baseball cap. A man's man by all indications, the kind of guy you might meet in a pool hall or hire to rebuild your deck.

"Shipment of cork dust came just in time, had plenty of colorant, made a boatload of berries last night."

What strange language was this fellow speaking? I didn't know how to respond, so I started back to the SUV to gather our gear.

"No need, got everything, wife made sandwiches. Mr. Pibb okay?"

I didn't realize there was another party joining us, but I nodded and got in his vehicle, a big, beat-up cruiser that would put a hitchhiker's thumb in his pocket. We lurched out of the parking lot and onto a north-south avenue in a run-down part of town. The trip proper had finally begun, and the Land Captain was at the helm. I liked the name, I wondered if he considered this car his boat. It certainly qualified as such. I was still trying to decide if I liked him or not.

As the engine gathered speed so did the conversation, or monologue rather. The job of a guide can be as simple as giving directions and often involves instruction. In some cases it can drift into entertainment, under the broader goal of showing people a good time. It was not clear that the Land Captain was purposely trying to provide this service, but he was doing a good job of it nonetheless. I admire people who speak their mind and let the chips fall where they may, and by that criterion the Land Captain and I were destined to be fast friends.

By the time we turned off the avenue and headed west we had keen insight into his nature and his personal life. Other than his cryptic remarks at introduction, fishing was apparently not a hot topic this morning. Instead, we learned of his position as head of the co-op board which was doing battle with a tyrannical landlord. His time in the service. And of greatest interest, how he came to do what he was doing now.

"Have you always been a Land Captain?" I asked with typical understated sarcasm.

"Nope. Sat behind a desk selling insurance for twenty years."

"That sounds like fun."

"It certainly wasn't," he answered, acknowledging my tendencies. "Put a gun in my mouth one night, thought about it, put the gun away. Went in the next morning, collected my stuff and left."

"No resignation of any kind?"

"Never said a word to my boss. Twenty years. Just left."

Sometimes the people who speak their minds can appear affable and approachable at first, and eventually turn out to be insane or dangerous. Or both. I wondered if I should reconsider my friendship criteria.

Fortunately, we were now approaching territory relevant to our quest. Something of a surprise, because we hadn't gotten too far. The Captain digressed from his autobiography to remark on the conditions as he leaned across the passenger side to peer at a canal that paralleled the road. There's water all over the place in Florida, so the canal hadn't seemed like anything special. Plus, in preparing for the trip I had the inner-city gondola ride in my mind, and we were in grassy, "placeless" land, a canal-divided boulevard slicing through suburban sprawl. But this was it and, although I was blind to them, evidently there were a host of visual clues present. A drive-by fishing forecast sprang from the Captain's mouth as we rolled along.

"Overcast, and the city's got the water running."

"Decent wind, berries should be falling."

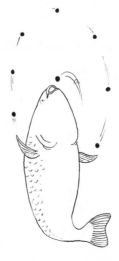

"There's one of them right past this intersection. There! See that, that's a berry tree."

We followed his gaze to the intermittent trees that clung to the shore. Isolated trees. Tight groups. Large. Small. They looked pretty much like magnolias and all looked the same. We'd traveled hundreds of miles and paid good money to drive along a roadside ditch with an insane person.

It would not be until well into the next day, on our own, that we would finally develop an eye for what the Land Captain was seeing. There was no other choice if we wanted to catch something. But right now we had the option of putting faith in our fearless leader. We pulled up to an open stretch opposite a stand of overhanging trees that were, for mysterious reasons, very appealing.

"See, there. No, not over there. RIGHT THERE!"

It sounded like El Capitan might get physical if we didn't catch on soon. So we concentrated harder and noticed that every few seconds, as the branches swayed, something was dropping into the water below. Berries. We didn't break out the rods, though, because nothing was eating them. If they're not surface-feeding, they're not feeding at all. Sinking berries, "wet" berries if you will, are not appetizing, we were told. Obviously.

The reconnaissance mission continued for several miles. Conditions pointed to a productive outing, but for some reason the fish were not holding up their end of the bargain.

"The water was boiling like Hell's Gate here yesterday."

I was waiting for that one. "Were they jumping in the boat?" I muttered to myself, getting antsy and irritated. It was now mid-morning and we hadn't even taken our rods out of the trunk yet. Captain Crunchberry sensed our growing unrest, particularly mine, so he switched gears and started on Peacock Bass, another inhabitant of the canal system. The Peacock Bass is brightly-colored and although small- and largemouth are technically members of the sunfish family, the peacock really does look like a larger, elongated pumpkinseed. We got a brief report on their tendencies and whereabouts and started scanning the shores. The canals receive influxes of water throughout the day at the discretion of the city. A supply line lay nearby and the Captain confirmed it as a good spot to try. The water was much deeper and the flow was churning up tons of debris from below in a lively boil. I threw out a streamer and started drawing it across the manmade current. I had lapsed into the stultified state that accompanies an outing marked for doom, when from the depths rose a fish such as I'd never seen. It was so big, so oversized for this body of water, and so close to me as it rolled over on the surface that I jumped back from the edge in fear. It was about the size of a human body and, based on what we'd seen thus far of modern-day Fort Lauderdale, I didn't doubt that's just what it was.

"Eighty-pound tarpon," announced the Land Captain. He deadpanned his proclamation, but there was an undertone of intense excitement. Now he was flying down the bank to see about hooking him.

"Cast again, CAST AGAIN!" he yelled at me as I stood there like I'd seen a ghost. I came out of it and tried to move my arms. "Oh my God!" I kept repeating as fear turned to determination. I *must* catch that thing. Or rather, I must hook that thing. I couldn't dream that I would actually land it. Who could, for that matter, using the puny fly rod I now held. Without warning the contest had shifted weight classes. It wasn't the first time, but nothing quite like this. What exactly *would* happen if by some miracle he got hooked? At the very least a pile-up on the street behind us as passersby watched the behemoth tail-dance his way down the canal.

Speculate though we did, it mattered little because we never saw him again. I cast into the roiling water over and over and over, replaying the encounter and wondering if there was something I could have done differently, even though I honestly don't believe he was going for my fly in the first place. Amid my disappointment there was a fresh, almost crazed twinkle in my eye. A heightened state of awareness about the wonders of Florida fishing. Peacocks? Grass carp? Offbeat or no, I didn't care where, how, why or who was or wasn't fishing for tarpon, this was a fish I wanted to get to know better.

The Land Captain, it turned out, is an accomplished tarpon fisherman. An accomplished fisherman period, for that matter. He was only too happy to oblige my sudden obsession. The canals may turn up a few strays, but as far inland as we were it was quite unusual. Hence his surprise and excitement over our earlier encounter. The Everglades were more popular stomping grounds for these prehistoric titans and it made sense, given our current location and shoreline limitations. It meant a decent hike cross-state. We bid farewell to the Sew-erz Canal for the time being and declared, "Go West, young men!"

Our guide revived his entertainment gig as we decompressed along I-75, an uninterrupted ribbon of desolation commonly known as Alligator Alley. The political incorrectness still flowed freely but he had ratcheted down a notch, perhaps owing to the fact that it was now past noon and our hands didn't smell. His content turned topical, first noting with disdain the collection of debris lining the fences and then the fences themselves, that flanked the highway. His interpretation was that they were erected to keep the "undesirables" from fishing, the side effect being that upstanding citizens of the fishing community such as ourselves were

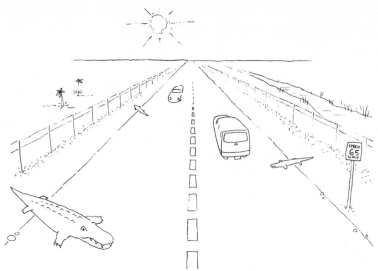

likewise barred. To us it seemed reasonable that if there had to be a highway cutting across, it need not be paved with alligator. Not to mention that having carloads of fishermen pulling off and on along this tropical autobahn was probably inadvisable from a safety standpoint. But we kept our opinions to ourselves as he switched his focus to Indians and then, at an inquiry from Seb, the sugar manufacturers.

"Sure, Big Sugar's screwed this area big time." I thought this might be a high-octane relative of Mr. Pibb (the South's version of Dr. Pepper I had learned), or possibly a rap star. It turned out to be a pejorative akin to "Big Tobacco." The sugar growers were conducting their business somewhere north of the highway and the Everglades, as they had for decades. Their practices had drawn increasing scrutiny from environmental groups and the issues had grown to statewide and national prominence.

"See those aqueducts headed north? That's for run-off, but there isn't much because Big Sugar's sucking the area dry. And what water does come this way is loaded with so much fertilizer it might as well stay where it is. Either way, it can't get through this freakin' highway-slash-dam, can it?"

As I learned more, I could see that this was not necessarily another conspiracy theory. Highway and Big Sugar both functioned to the detriment of the Everglades. Yet man had arrived and he wasn't leaving, and here we were using the highway to our benefit to reach the tarpon kingdom. I had sweetened my coffee this morning. And Mr. Pibb well, he's probably responsible for any number of endangered species. Again I opted to zip it.

Midway across we stopped where a subtle depression in the fence made access difficult but possible. The high sun beat down mercilessly

as we consumed the Land Lady's tasty sandwiches and sipped our Mr.
Pibb while silently surveying our host's latest selection–another segment of canal, one that couldn't possibly have tarpon as it was even
smaller water than the last. But it had plenty of vegetation abutting and
atop the water and looked promising for other species. The cruiser's
pitted roof rack held a canoe which now came off and into play. In
classic offbeat fashion we hoisted it over the fence and slid it in the
water. Three grown men hovering around 200 pounds each makes for
some precarious canoeing. Mix in the fact that you're operating beside
a highway named for a man-eating reptile and you have all the mak-
ings of a dark comedy-horror flick. There was a gator or two in sight at
all times. Cap noted the cuts through the brush as prime gator tunnels:
exercise caution. A six-footer slamming his tail a rod's length from the
boat provided the exclamation point. I leaned forward to hug the
Captain but thought better of it.

Word had come down that this
place was a "guarantee." For what I
didn't know, I had inquired about
bass and was told tersely that, yes,
bass were in here. I really liked the
name "Big Sugar" and couldn't let
go of it. I decided that a hefty

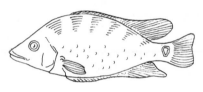

Mayan Cichlid

Florida largemouth would hereafter be called a Sugar Bass. Fat and
sweet. But the time of day made me skeptical that I'd meet up with
one. Still, I would be content with any member of the sunfish family at
this point. Even a bream, like Seb was just now pulling up. He hooked
another and a third. The way things had been going, it really was a
welcome relief to have something to reel in, and the water was fun to
fish: lots of overhanging brush and opportunities for short, accurate
casts as we paddled by. The sunfish shared space with the Mayan
Cichlid, an aptly-bizarre name for a non-indigenous fish introduced via
the contents of someone's discarded aquarium. Tilapia too. The edge
came off as we did battle with a variety pack of colorful aliens.

After a while I stopped fishing and started simmering again. The
sun had moved to a point where you subconsciously feel the day winding down. A lot of people who don't fish share a derisive view of fishing as a non-athletic sport where you sit on your butt all day drinking
and watching your line, then make up stories as you swerve home.
Though perhaps not athletic in the full sense, when you fish as Seb and
I do you're pretty well spent by the end of an outing. And as age
creeps up, that feeling comes on earlier. The hot weather certainly
played a part. Either way, I was starting to get a bit weary as we
reloaded the canoe and made for the 'Glades.

The Land Captain may have been getting a little weary too. He had been around longer than we, but was probably in better shape owing to his career of choice. We heard a single, rousing tale about extracting a treble hook from the stomach and through the neck of an overzealous heron while angling for snook in the inner lakes of the Everglades. But now I noticed his delivery was ebbing. I couldn't imagine that he had run out of material, maybe this was the part of the trip where he usually waxes poetic about the day's glories. "That Tilapia ran with your line like an FSU fullback headed for a sorority mixer." Wouldn't quite cut it. Seb and I picked up the ball instead, telling him a bit about our backgrounds and occupations. My D.C. counterpart is also well-versed on issues affecting the fishing industry nationwide, including the Everglades. The Cap made for a restless listener and sought to opine. But Seb had launched into a full-fledged fishing filibuster and would brook no interruption. At times I wonder whether he imagines a video monitor is pointed at him as he auditions for *The Reel World.* I rolled down the windows to release the heat.

The western horizon grew redder as we reached the end of the interminable Alley and pulled into a gas station to refuel; a routine practice elsewhere which, if neglected in an environment such as this, could result in death. According to the Cap, a wrong turn might also prove fatal. And he wasn't talking about alligators or heat stroke. We hadn't noticed but a quick review confirmed the presence of man but a disturbing lack of civilization. The convenience mart was the cultural mecca for these parts. A mile or so down the road we pulled off to the shoulder beside a short concrete bridge low to the water. An inlet traveled under the bridge and between mid-span piers of tubular concrete. Very steep banks. Again, small water, but deep. Maybe I didn't have a good feel for the type of water these tarpon preferred. The Captain noted that he'd caught plenty of keepers right here, a few that tore out the other side of the bridge and into the backing. We had spent enough time with him to know that he was colorful but not given to embellishment or B.S.

"Sounds good, but how exactly does one cast here?" we wanted to know.

"Ah, that is the question, isn't it?" he replied, and removed a rod from the trunk to demonstrate.

The road we had taken and now shouldered was the Tamiami Trail, another east-west conduit and the equivalent of Route 1, the local passage along the Northeast Coast. Just as I-95 had taken the pressure off route 1, Alligator Alley now bore the main traffic burden here. Still, plenty of cars whizzed by above, and there were phone lines as well. Throw in the underpass, the likely whereabouts for a lurking tarpon and the fly's improbable destination, and it made for an Extreme Sports fly fishing challenge. Captain Land had been training and was a formidable opponent. Positioned at the top of the bank, he started casting out and back but also up and down, generating length and power without yet addressing the underpass. This also avoided the nearby cars and wires. Once he had enough going on, he rotated the directionality and shot a picture-perfect cast a good two-thirds of the way under the bridge. Amazing! An experience found only in fly fishing, where the technique is arguably more rewarding than the results.

"Now you guys try it," he said, raising the rod above and behind his head for the next willing contestant. Seb looked at me and I shook my head. He stepped onto the bank for a lesson in humility. Since Seb does a lot more fly fishing than I do, he's less willing to take advice or criticism. LC had noticed this and was browbeating him. For God's sake, I thought, how could someone who hadn't done this before possibly get it right the first time? The Captain had probably cast here thousands of times. Besides, aesthetics were nice but there was the bottom line to consider, and by now Seb had put a few pretty deep in the tunnel. The competition was heating up, but the sun was going down. The underpass was getting a low reading on my mental tarpon-o-meter, so we moved along.

An inlet canal directly off the ocean provided the day's final setting. Less cover and the wind had picked up. It would pose a casting problem. With the finish line in sight, we summoned our remaining energies for one final push. Our side of the inlet was an arid expanse of baked grass with heavy vegetation at shore only. Wind aside, a fly-friendly arrangement. The other shore had some midscale ranch homes with piers and reeds. The mightiest of casts might span the distance, but was unnecessary since there was surface activity throughout the deep channel. We stood at a cut in the brush and assessed the variously subtle and ferocious disturbances.

"All tarpon," came a voice from the other side. A park ranger living in one of the houses had come down to tend to his boat.

"This place is basically an aquarium, it's got hundreds of tarpon, some into triple digits in weight. But they're savvy, I wouldn't get too excited just yet."

The Land Captain deafly handed us our rods and we began tossing flies that looked like white Muddler Minnows in the direction of the feeding.

"Guy probably sits on his dock all day plunking crabs. The bigger the tarpon, the smaller the bait. You can't beat flies for these babies."

I wanted to believe him. I was saying a little prayer to myself. It was

now or never. A silvery flash and a good-size fish sideswiped the tail end of my retrieve. He was on for a split second, then gone. That was it, my one and only chance. Gloom and doom started descending again. This time I fought back. Disgusted, yet I had to admit that my first-ever tarpon strike was itself a thrill. They were quick, and so silky-smooth. Appeared out of nowhere, traveling at a high speed, then rolled sideways as they struck so you got a really good look at them even when they didn't break water. It was spellbinding.

A few moments later Seb had a similar opportunity and made the most of it. He landed a nice fish, tarpon number one in the O'Kelly record book. I was self-absorbed in mental fish-games and took scant notice. Soon I was devising a plan. Alligator Alley was long when one was chugging across in a rusty cruiser. Sidestep the Mayan fields and with my lead foot I bet I could cut the trip in half. We had a few days left, plenty of time to make any number of new friends: grass carp, peacock bass, why not a certain stealth bomber from the Everglades?

I managed a smile as I walked over to see about Seb's triumph. I hadn't caught a tarpon, but the good news was this: I knew now that I would.

Peasants, Kings, and Ants from Hell

By Sebastian O'Kelly

A heavy state of ennui has settled over Chris and I. Perhaps it is the come down from the high of my first-ever tarpon, now caught more than a day past. It could be the sight, as we drive the streets of Fort Lauderdale, of strip shopping center and after strip shopping center, heavily populated with all the national chain stores and franchises and completely devoid of local character, that leaves us with the depressing thought that we are at the crossroads of Everytown and Anytown, U.S.A. But most likely it is the leaden sky and one and a half inches of rain that has been dumped in the area and completely blown out the day's fishing. We are more than halfway through our trip and feel that we have barely broken the surface of the waters of South Florida.

We try to make something of the day–a stop at the International Game Fish Association museum to learn some fishing history; a stroll down the packed aisles of Bass Pro Shop's Outdoor World to pick up some new stuff; and a late lunch at a café in South Beach to watch the Beautiful People, their best features unfortunately covered in rain gear, stroll by. These events, while interesting all, cannot put our mission back on track and displace our current state of resignation. It only can be mended by our fix of choice and need–fishing.

Thankfully, the morning of the third day, while not exactly blooming bright, wasn't overflowing storm drains or blowing down billboards. We

would get our fix and our spirits lifted with the clouds. We fueled up at
a greasy spoon and drove to a canal
east of the airport. We idled along
the canal looking for trees ripe with
ficus berries before coming to a big
and obvious selection. The wind
was still, the berries were falling,
and, best of all, fish were swirling to
eat them! I readied my 8-weight
with one of the Land Captain's
berry flies. The dilemma arose–fish
on the same side of the tree and have shorter casts but spook the fish
more easily, or go to the far bank and face long casts and a little–and I
emphasize "little"–less chance of spooking them. We opted to go to
the other side, knowing long casts also meant being careful not to
hook the four-wheeled, high-speed fighters passing behind us. Either
way we would face the challenge of bull's-eyeing the fly into tight
gaps between the tree branches hanging low over where the fish lay.

Our target was the grass carp, more properly know as the white
amur, and like most of Florida's residents, a transplant from elsewhere–
in this case from Asia and brought in especially by the state's fish man-
agers to control noxious weed growth that clogs water pipes, asphyxi-
ates other fish and has non-native species advocates in such a snit that
they are willing to introduce another non-native species to deal with
the out-of-town green goop. And deal with it these fellows can, reportedly being able to munch their weight in hydrilla and milfoil in a day.
Amur are big and fast growers overall, capable of reaching 100 pounds
in their home waters on the other side of the world and about half that
size in these canals. To make sure their numbers don't get out of hand,
only barren fish–known as triploids in scientificese–are stocked. The
biologists sterilize the fish through a handy bit of genetic engineering
(by temperature shocking the eggs) at the hatchery. This causes them
to create an additional chromosome that results in infertility.

The better-known common, or European, carp is also an introduced
species in U.S. waters, an effort some decades ago to provide a food
fish for subsistence fishermen and working-class folks. But that fact,
along with the sharing of the name and like dime-sized scales on the
flanks, is where the similarity ends. The grass carp is actually a member
of the minnow family, a gigantic vegetarian one at that, a testament of
what can happen to you little fishes if you eat all your spinach. It is
longer and more streamlined than the European carp and doesn't have
the tell-tale barbels on the underside of its mouth. The amur is also far

more eco-friendly. It doesn't cloud the water and muddy the bottom like the pig-rooting common carp, nor does it consume fish eggs. Best of all, in munching all those weeds, it saves our waterways from the dumping of literally tons of toxic plant control chemicals and herbicides.

As far as we know, the Land Captain is the only person to make a go at fishing for grass carp (within the fly fishing biz). Why haven't we heard more about them? Perhaps the fishery is still in its pioneering phase, but I suspect the old class thing among desirable species–"the carp is a trash fish, Sir Godfrey! I'm in total agreement, Lightibbets."–is at work here. There may also be fishing ego at play too. These are not easy fish. It is one thing to be humbled by the speedy bonefish or splendid steelhead. But to be spurned by the lowly amur? I can't see too many fly fishers taking the risk or expense to fish for them and then having to tell their buds at the local TU chapter how they got skunked.

Back to the canal and our berry-loving friends. Every once in awhile, I have a fishing day where Murphy's Law fully and forcefully applies. These are days when the gear inexplicably fails, the line always seems to tangle, the casts are just a little off target, the guy fishing next to me catches fish after fish while I am getting none, yet he is seemingly using the same techniques, and lastly when I finally manage a hit or two I strike a split-second too early or too late. There isn't a fisherman out there, even among the experts, who hasn't had at least some days like these. When I was younger, I used to get pretty irate, curses would fly, condemnations would spill forth with the occasional fishing box flung upon the ground. I wasn't quite John McEnroe with a fishing rod (I was too poor to replace any broken rods) but I used to get quite pissed. I've mellowed some since then. The Murphy's Law days haven't entirely gone away, nor my frustration at going through one, but I have come to recognize them as temporary states to gut through before the Fishing God would once again find favor with me and bless my line.

Today was proving such a day. My first casts were tentative and not in feeding range. Then, when shooting line for longer shots, it would catch on these brambly-looking plants in the short grass. I finally made a near-perfect cast but it was off by a few inches and snagged in a ficus tree branch. Next, I stepped on a bed of fire ants, which had me hopping around slapping my sandaled feet for the next few minutes. All the while, big carp sloshed and slapped at the real thing falling on the water in front of us. I finally got a few good drifts but no takes. I switched to 3X, the Land Captain's suggest-

ed tippet size, shot in a good cast, got a hit and snapped it off. Then I
stepped on another ant nest. More jumping around. My curses were
showing real edge now. We went over to the other side to try to wig-
gle up to the fish on our bellies and dap the fly in front of them with
only a few inches of line extending from the rod tip. I slowly maneuvered into position, all the while telling Chris that with this short
amount of line it was important to wait for the fish to fully take before
setting the hook. Sure enough, the self-anointed expert ignores his own
advice. I lower the fly in the water, a carp strikes and I yank the fly
right out of his mouth. A Charlie Brown-like "aaagh!" spills from my
mouth.

My exasperation was playing out in front of fish that would brook
no fishing sin. I could sense that these overgrown minnows, these so-
called peasants of the fish world were, in an interesting role reversal,
laughing at me and talking trash. 'Hey there, big clod, we can see you
and if we can see you, we won't feed for at least five minutes until
you're gone. That berry there, it looks like it's dragging in the current a
little bit—sorry, we don't eat those and we certainly won't go out of our
way to eat one that's a foot outside our feeding lane. And the next one
—we may eat a berry with a sprig attached for fiber content and
improved digestion but what do you have tied to it this time? That tippet looks as thick as steel cable—nice try!. I see you threw one into the
tree and can't get it back—aww, poor baby! Nah, nah, nah-nah, you
traveled over 1,000 miles and you can't catch us!'

We head back over to the other side. We've been alternating turns
with the rod (the commotion associated with two people fishing simultaneously would scare these fish across to the other side of Florida)

and now I'm frustrated enough to let Chris do most of it. While they haven't been jumping all over his berry flies either, his encounters with the ants and tangled line have been less troublesome and his mood has stayed positive. Our movement away from the near bank has the carp feeding more freely now. They are sloshing everywhere and while they are difficult to see under the glare and dark water, every now and then a husky, brown form reveals itself at the surface like a wallowing hippo. They are big, ten, fifteen, and even twenty pounds, the Shaq Daddy Diesels of the canal world.

Chris makes the best cast of the day and lays the berry through a PC monitor-sized gap in the branches where it softly touches down at the shadowy edge of the canopy. It drifts for a second before disappearing in a swirl. He lifts the rod—fish on! He gets the beefy amur on the reel quickly as it makes a couple of strong runs in the middle of the canal before slowing. I scramble down the bank to perform the landing duties but as Chris gets the fish close, it gets a glimpse of us and rips back into the middle. The amur plays this game a couple of more times before fully tiring. I hoist him from the water, his body thick and cool in my hands—into double digits for sure—and hand him over to Chris for a Kodak moment. Chris then guides him back to his home.

Chris's success has energized me somewhat but I still feel some bad juju stalking me. I cast anyway and sure enough the brambly things, despite an impromptu manual mow of the area by my partner, raise their prickly heads again to snag my line. Then I step on my third ant hill. Enough is enough. At this point, it's time to pull back, regroup, massage my wounded fishing ego, rub salve into those ant bites, and kick Murphy's Law in the butt and out of my fishing day. We agree to stop at a supermarket to pick up some cold cuts, look for a Wal-mart to buy a plastic bin to serve as a fort against the bramblies, and then head back to the hotel to put some sneakers on. While walking the supermarket aisles, Chris pulls a cantaloupe out of a cardboard box and puts the box in the cart.

"You can put it in this," he states.

"Huh?" I look at him dully, thinking he is referring to an alternative to paper or plastic.

"So the line doesn't tangle."

I shake the dimness from my head. Of course. The box is the perfect size and more durable and heavier than it first appears. It is even covered with a wax-like finish which looks like it would repel water in all but the heaviest downpour. A freebie and a saved trip to the ubiquitous Wal-mart to boot—what a perfect find!

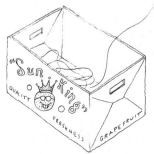

We return to the hotel but damned if I can't find my sneakers. I
look everywhere, under the bed, in the bathroom, in the trash (in case
the maid made an executive decision about shoes that should have
been so retired a long time ago). No go. Chris asks if I left them in the
car. I tell him I looked earlier but double-check anyway. I search more
throughly and–lo and behold–the stinkers are hidden behind a couple
of plastic bags in the rear. I peer at the red welts on my feet and ankles
and think about the 90 percent that wouldn't be there if I actually
applied what got me through one of the top colleges in the country,
though that was nearly 20 years ago and before the onset of mid-life
confusion that has me struggling to execute the most minimal activities,
like figuring out voice mail on my cell phone, required of modern life.

It's back on the concrete path to the canal, eating sammies on the fly.
We are traveling quickly–Chris likes to nail the accelerator to the base-
board, a consistent 85-90 mph while on the highway–and I hope we are
moving quickly enough to leave Murphy and his bad juju behind. I close
my eyes and take a few deep breaths. I'm trying to reach that fish/no
fish zen state of mind that will flush the morning's negativity away. I can
smell the oil from the road. The bumps of the tarmac jar my body. The
sound of whizzing autos is everywhere. Motoring in the urban environment is not the place to get down with serious meditation, but the short
respite from the fishing and some grub in an empty tummy at least has
me feeling upbeat and ready to take on the amur again.

We reach our favorite tree and park on the far bank. We take a little more time to study the fish. They're more spread out than in the morning and several are feeding just down current of the tree. It looks like the near bank might be better so it's back over to the other side. I ready the rod and get in position, the freebie stripping box at my feet. I look for fire ant hills to smoosh in an act of vengeance with my now besocked and sneakered feet. It's funny how the nasty little critters can't be found when the advantage swings to the human. It would be funnier still if the state, employing the hydrilla-to-grass carp model, allowed the import of non-indigenous African anteaters as part of a fire ant eradication campaign.

As it is, it appears that the pest control authorities have heard not only my call for fire ant eradication, but that of hundreds of thousands of other people who have been stung (and the few that have died from allergic reactions); of those who have seen their houses go up in flames (fire ants have a peculiar affinity for electricity and shorting out circuit boxes); of the millions of baby birds, reptiles (some experts believe that fire ants have decimated the horned toad population in Texas) and mammals stung to death in their nests; and of the countless local ant species wiped out from competition.

But you won't actually see a four-foot anteater rummaging through your garbage anytime soon. In fact, you won't see this dedicated fire ant enemy at all. But with a very close look you might see one that could prove even more effective. Scientists with the U.S. Department of Agriculture are now experimenting with the release of flea-sized fliers from Latin America called phorid flies that strike fear in the hearts and, more relevantly, heads of fire ants everywhere.

Their means of attack is to descend upon the milling ants and strike with the precision of laser guided bombs, implanting an egg in the abdomen with a harpoon-like appendage called an ovipositor before the ant can retaliate against the unwanted piggy-backer. The egg hatches into a tiny maggot which worms its way through the ant's insides and into the ant's head (bet that feels good). As it reaches the head, the maggot secretes a decapitating enzyme which dissolves the con-necting tissue between the body and the head. The head subsequently rolls off and the remaining ants, for some strange reason, collect it and place it in a pile with all the others. Safe inside the hard chitinous shell, the maggot feeds on the brain and jaw muscles until it is ready to hatch into an adult. Then the cycle repeats itself.

There are fire ants in Latin America, but the phorids do a pretty job of keeping their population down. Apparently, the flies make head cases out of the ants in more ways than one. Researchers have discov-

ered that when phorids are nearby, ant activity slows. They don't venture out of the nest as much to search for food or to destroy other ants.
They pile on top of each other, hide more, basically hunker down in
fear and develop a bunker-type mentality so-to-speak. I am a fan of
psyching out these ants but as I look at the growing pustules on my
feet, it is the phorids' decapitational skills I admire most.

My presentation on the first few casts is not quite good enough and
I don't find any takers. But I remain calm. Then, there's a disturbance
in the open water away from the tree. Then another and another, in
what looks like a free-for-all, a berry jamboree, with the amur abandoning previous caution in a smorgasbord of berries and jockeying among
themselves for the best feeding position. I shoot a delicate cast close,
and almost as soon as it hits the water it disappears. I rear back–fish
on! The carp bull rushes into the middle of the canal. I let him run. He
zags downstream. Then I pump him back. We go back and forth, give
and take, for five minutes. I bring him close. We see him, he see us –
he splits. This happens a half-dozen times, before he calls it quits and
Chris hikes down to bring him in. I hold the amur, well over 10
pounds I conclude, for the proverbial glossy, then let him go.

It is a great feeling to have the grass carp juju finally banished. Chris
looks pleased for the both of us. But he has a faraway look in his eyes
and I sense immediately what it is. A metallic glint flashes across them
as bright as the scales of the Silver King. There is still plenty of day left
and the mighty tarpon is calling to us from across the Everglades.

As we eat up miles along I-75 I start thinking about what many consider the greatest of our gamefish. Our original mission hadn't been to
pursue tarpon. It had been more of "let's get down there, see what we
see, and try for some of these unusual species in atypical places." The
traditional fishing Grand Slam of tarpon, permit, and bonefish was not
what we were after. Tarpon in my mind had always been something of
an unattainable catch, beyond my skill–at least with the fly rod–and
certainly beyond my means. And all the stories I heard about them,
particularly the bigger ones, entailed paying some Type-A Florida Keys
guide $600 a day (tip included) to yell at you for the chance, if you
were lucky and the tarpon were willing, of jumping one or two fish and
maybe, just maybe, hitting roulette wheel-type odds and actually landing one, in which case, back at the dock, the guide would get all the
credit and he would use any pics of the fish as part of his marketing
brochure. You'd end up as just a proverbial notch in his fly rod case.
My friend Mark, more affectionately known as Tearjerker, squires some
wealthy law firm clients of his for a trip each year where he burns a
good chunk of those $400 an hour fees chasing these fish. I don't think
he's caught one yet, but I know he has jumped several, which in the

world of tarpon fishing is considered almost as good as a catch. That sort of high-end, super-competitive, fishing for hours on end for a brief moment of connection with a fish, no matter how spectacular it might be, just wasn't Chris's and my bag.

Still, I've always held some fascination with tarpon. Start with its scientific name, *Megalops atlanticus*–how cool a name is that? M-e-g-a-l-o-p-s. Sounds big, very mysterious, a little scary even–all adjectives that those in the know use to describe the fish. My experience has been limited to the written word, the occasional ESPN Outdoors show, and the day with the Land Captain. Still, I've researched them enough to have heard that the basic evolution of these Alpha predators has not changed in 125 million years, dating back to the Cretaceous period, yet man knows little about them. They are found in tropical climes in the Gulf of Mexico and the South Atlantic, along the Mexican Coast down to Central America, and on the West Coast of Africa where the current all-tackle record of 283 pounds was caught off Senegal. They are long-lived. One scientist–by dating the rings of the otoliths in the tarpon's ear, a process not unlike aging trees by counting the rings in their trunks–estimated the age of a 220-pound female at 78 years. They are considered migratory but little is known about the details of their travels. A conservation group called Bonefish-Tarpon Unlimited has been raising funds to plant satellite tags in mature tarpon to track their movements in a real-time manner. It's important work, but at $3,000 a pop, the tagging is expensive and so far has been limited to tagging of only a few fish. I wonder if the spy mavens at the Department of Defense had any idea that a derivation of their Cold War invention would one day be used to track fish patterns and migration.

There are other unique and fascinating features about tarpon. For years, scientists thought they came inshore to spawn during the late spring and early summer. Juveniles would feed and grow in the mangrove swamps and canals in the Everglades and along the Southwest Coast of Florida until they reached adult size, generally considered about 60 pounds or so, and headed out into the open ocean to become migratory. Spawning was presumably preceded by an event called "daisy-chaining" where a pod of tarpon swim nose-to-tail in a lazy circle or figure 8 type formation in shallow water.

But it turns out that tarpon actually spawn far offshore at distances of almost 125 miles from land. Currents sweep the microscopic larvae to shore and back into the mangroves where the juveniles grow as the scientists had earlier surmised. As for the "daisy chaining", no one is really sure why tarpon exhibit such an elaborate maneuver of underwater tail-gating. What is known is that the species is capable of living in almost any watery environment–fresh, salt, brackish, flowing, still–

provided that it stays warm. Tarpon can even survive in the most stagnant, oxygen-deprived waters, places that would asphyxiate almost any
other kind of fish. They accomplish this through an air bladder that
allows them to gulp air just above the surface and get their oxygen fix
that way instead of through the gills. When tarpon roll at the surface,
it's often to fill their bladder, though they can be trying to suck in baitfish up top as well.

The Silver Kings are calling and as royal subjects, Chris and I are
obeying. The other day I saw, albeit in a downsized way, why that title
would apply. My tarpon did all the things a fighting fish is supposed to
do—he jumped, he sprinted, he rolled, he bulldogged, he tried to break
my line off in the weeds, he shook his head, and maybe most importantly, he never quit. Normally, if you can find a species who will do
two of the above, you have found a fighting fish. But all of the above,
that is indeed a rare fish. Others suggest the title comes from the size
of an adult fish and the way it appears suddenly, ghost-like in the shallow water of the flats, its silver dollar-sized eye peering up at you
through the film, colors of silver, lavender and green flashing in the
reflective sunlight, massive jaw flexing in a bucket-sized woosh of water
as a hapless baitfish is engulfed. Then with a mighty stroke of its tail,
the tarpon disappears into the aquamarine, all the while you are staring
in awe and have forgotten to lift your rod to cast, much to the chagrin
of your tourney-winning guide who has been yelling, "10 o'clock, 90
feet—he's a good one....Get ready....9 o'clock, 60 feet....Cast, c'mon,
cast....30 feet!...Cast, god dammit, cast....He's right there!...Shit, he's
gone." And you haven't heard a word the entire time.

If you happen to overcome the initial deer-in-headlights reaction to
actually make a cast and the Silver King is so benevolent as to deign to
accept your offering and you are mindful enough to have a super-sharp
hook that actually pierces then holds that titanium-reinforced jaw, then
the next thing you will mostly likely experience—aside from the ear-
whining sound of a screeching reel and the pain of a busted knuckle if
you've carelessly left your hand too close to its handle—is the magnificent sight of his emergence from the water in silver-plated armor, body
twisting and turning, spiraling in a fury before crashing down and bar-
reling toward the open sea, making a number of catapulting jumps
along the way. If you forget for a moment during one of these
Jordanesque leaps that you are in the presence of such a ruler and do
not pay your respects by bowing both your body and rod tip toward
him, you will rudely be punished by a busted line and a fish swimming
free in the other direction. That's because if the line is kept taut, as is
typically taught when fishing for most species in order to maintain tension on the hook, there is a good possibility the tarpon will roll over

during his leap and land right on the line when he hits the water and snap it instantly. If you bow and put some slack in the line, then it should absorb the shock of his leap and landing. So bow down and humble yourself before the King!

We reach the Everglades and the canal where I had caught my tarpon. They are rolling again on the surface and over against the far bank something (or somethings) big are creating a rippling disturbance in the reeds. There is not as much activity as before but there is enough going on to catch our breath and hurry us to get the rods rigged. No wind is working against us and I am soon booming casts across the canal and retrieving my slider with alternating steady and erratic strips. The only critter putting a crimp in the activity are steady numbers of deer- and horseflies that land on my shoulders just out of swatting range. But they prove far less of a distraction than the morning's fire ants.

I power out lots of casts and move around to a few different spots but find no takers. That's O.K. It feels good just to make some long casts. The sun has finally come out through late afternoon clouds and the temperature is a perfect 80. Then I hear some splashes. I hurry over to where Chris is standing, his rod bent into a fish. A Silver King has knighted him with a take! The tarpon shoots out of the water again.

"He's got the hops!" I exclaim.

Chris manages only a tight-lipped smile. After losing a tarpon two days ago, he is not going to exhibit any pre-catch celebration. The fish hops some more and rips out line. Chris brings him close before he makes another run. I move to the water's edge. I'm a little nervous. I don't want to screw up the landing of Chris's first tarpon. But he gets him close and I manage to get a thumb under the lip and pull him skyward. He's a juvenile but has proven himself worthy of the lineage. Chris caught him on his 6-weight trout rod, something not recommended in the Orvis catalog ("our 6-weight superlight fluor-doro-boro composite derived from Stealth fighter plane technology will fit your hand perfectly for that day on the Delaware when you need both finesse and presentation to fool those difficult 18-inch rainbows"), but both he and equipment performed ably in light of the power of the fish. We burn the memory into film and back in the water the young prince goes.

We fish for an hour more, then stop on the way back at a bassy tank of water by the highway that proves unproductive. It shows all signs of being heavily fished—coils of line in the grass, heavily trod banks, empty Styrofoam worm containers strewn about—and the only hit I get is near a sunken fridge. On the ride back, I give the Land Captain a call to give him a report on our challenging, but ultimately satisfying, day of fishing. I knew we had done him proud and like most

good guides, he would be happy to hear our report even though he hadn't been present.

His response is typical Land Captain, metaphoresque with a little non-sequitur added in. "Ah, the greater glories of Athens were realized on the bloody plains of Marathon."

The next day dawns gray. The sky looks like it will bucket at any second. But we resolve to squeeze a closing couple of hours of angling before my flight departs and Chris rockets north in the trusty Explorer. It showers while we eat breakfast at the nearby greasy spoon and we try to keep our eyes on the food instead of on a young lady with a tight Hooters T-top and bait-bucket-sized, and obviously equally as plastic, breasts.

We want to fish some of these ponds tucked between the interchanges of the confluence of I-595 and I-95 that we'd seen from the road. First though, we try a lake at an urban park that the Land Captain has recommended. The water looks weedy and appropriately fishy if a little off-color. But we see little fish activity and get no hits on our offerings. The highlight of the visit comes when I find the biggest fire ant hill I'd ever seen and take out my revenge with a dirt-gouging and hill-leveling branch. If only there had been a few phorids around...free larva food everywhere!

We leave to explore one of the ponds, more like a small lake really, at the highway interchange. We pull the car off an exit ramp and wait out another shower. The water looks even more inviting up close. There's tall grass and some cattails along the banks and the shallows ripple with small baitfish before falling off into deep water. Still, it's strange to be fishing here. I know it's an overused word, but surreal would be the right term. Highways, byways, skyways, cloverleafs, on- and off-ramps, loop all around us in a concrete spaghetti maze that looks as if it could have served as a backdrop for the Jetsons if Hollywood had ever done a non-animated version. Chris remarks that this elaborate twisting of roads could never have been designed before the computer age. Cars and trucks rattle and speed by. I worry that it won't be long before the Highway Patrol pulls over and waves us away, or worse, writes us a hefty fine. But none do and my worries are calmed a good deal when we see a sign that prohibits boating and swimming but is quiet on our favorite hobby, thereby implicitly per- mitting it. Allowed or not, it's clear we are among the pioneers at try- ing this spot. There is no fishing detritus anywhere. This spot is reserved for the offbeat.

It is not long after a few casts that I hook and release a small large- mouth. Then I see Chris up ahead with a rod bent into a good fish. He has switched to spinning gear with a rubber worm. I hustle over. He pulls in his catch after one or two nice jumps.

"It's a peacock bass," he says, lipping it like a largemouth. The fish has brilliant, dappled hues of color. The bottom of his belly is yellow, which turns to a fiery orange further up the flank before melting into a light olive and darkening into green along the top. Three black, inky stripes run perpendicular on its side. It's a vibrantly colorful fish, sort of like what a largemouth would look like on an acid trip.

"Cool." I reach into my pack and snap another one for the album before he lets it go.

"He was nesting over here," Chris notes, pointing to spot close to shore. "It was like how the Land Captain described. I dragged the worm past his nose and he jumped on it."

Peacocks are another non-indigenous species and, like the grass carp, have been deliberately planted by fisheries officials in South Florida, though strictly for the enjoyment of the angler as these South American imports, like their northern cousin and last name namesake, are carnivores. They spawn at this time of year in shallow beds along the bank and the local fishing wisdom has it that, even though they have other things on the brain besides food, they can usually be induced to bite by repeatedly dragging a fly or lure by or into their nest. Their hot Latin blood usually gets the best of them and they eventually strike after an offering has been dropped into their nest for the umpteenth time.

We catch a couple more small largemouths. We fish quickly as my flight-time is soon, though it is clear to us that we haven't found a major hawg hole. There are three or four other lakes at various other off- ramps in the interchange and one of them could be the mother lode.

But they'll have to wait for another trip. Chris drops me at the airport. I hurry to board and sit next to an older woman.

I think back on our trip. Collectively, we caught an exotic species or better yet, given both the fish and human demographics of the region, an immigrant Grand Slam of white amur, Mayan cichlids and peacock bass. And we both caught our first tarpon, an achievement in the fish-

ing world akin to one's first kiss. Our quarry spanned the fishing socio-economic spectrum in that class-free way we like to fish. We explored interesting waters and scouted others to come back to. We discussed bringing Chris's kayak next time to really get back into some of the 'Glades's canals, provided we had a plan to avoid getting hopelessly lost, munched by alligators, or devoured by insects. Speaking of the latter, I made sure to keep my legs thrust all the way under the seat during the whole trip.

No need to end a perfectly good trip by having the lady next to me reach for the vomit bag at the sight of my blistered, ant-ravaged feet.

New York Revisited

By Christopher Arelt

I never considered myself a real New Yorker. There are degrees of New York, you see, as anyone from the big city will tell you. For instance, I was born and raised on Long Island, but pretty far out. And I don't even live in New York State now, I live in Connecticut, which to a Manhattanite is a little farther than upstate but not as far as New Jersey. Spent some time in Park Slope, Brooklyn, my best shot at induction, but that was for only five years. Transient status at best. You see my point.

Or do you? How can I explain this to a broader audience? Maybe through an event. Take the 1987 Superbowl. Did anyone, *anywhere*, really consider Bills-Giants a battle of two New York teams? Maybe the folks in Buffalo, which although it's technically part of the state is not like…the Meadowlands? Bad example. I know, the 2000 Subway Series, Mets and Yankees. First time in forty-someodd years, since 'dem Bums split for fun in the sun. Now *that's* New York. Except, Shea Stadium is located well into Long Island, and everyone from my far-flung hometown rooted for the Mets, and…wait! I've just figured it out. Obviously it's not about whether you live in NY State. But it's not as simple as the five boroughs of NY City either. It's whether, at some point in your life, ideally since birth or for a minimum duration of, I'd say, twenty years, you received mail at a location visible on the New York Transit Authority map of the mass transit system. You know, the one on the subways. That solves the Shea Stadium dilemma because, as John Rocker will tell you (if you can find him), the #7 train runs there. Surely that's the standard, if you're on the map for twenty-plus, you're in. Congrats!

Make no mistake, the real thing is a special breed, a highly-evolved product of the ultimate in urban environments. Imposters are exposed in a New York minute. As a self-described pseudo-New Yorker, I've had plenty of first-hand experience from which to develop a deep understanding and respect. For instance I remember, fresh out of college, standing in a lunch line at a deli in midtown. When I reached the front, I paused to select a sandwich from the chalkboard. The guy behind the counter stares at me for about a half a second and when I don't say anything, he beckons past and starts doing business with the woman behind me. A lesson learned, the first of many. A tough place. But also a great place. Activity, creativity, diversity. A 24/7 celebration of life.

Yet if I'd remained in Park Slope all these years, I'd be verging on citizenship by now. The truth is, I never got comfortable there. I like the option of solitude, the outdoor variety to be exact. That's a big part of fishing for me and always has been. See some creatures others don't. Escape the sounds of car, plane, power equipment. Heed nature's call at a moment's notice. Prospect Park might provide certain of these opportunities, but it's not the same. Of course the city's beautiful, but it's not natural beauty, or at least I thought not until recently. And so as I venture back into the big city to say a little bit about fishing there, I know I'd better offer some prop's in the way of this lengthy preamble. Because when it comes to fishing in the Big Apple, the truth may be, "I don't know *nuthin.*"

One thing I do know, quite well, is the aforementioned subway map. We became close, you might say, during the late '80s when my face was pressed up against it each morning inside a cattle car called the F-train. I love maps, and under the transistor-like maze of multi-colored train routes lay the pale, abstracted backdrop of the city's geography. I studied it daily. First off, I realized that Brooklyn was actually located on Long Island. And there was the mysterious Island of Staten. Unbeknownst to me at the time, the home of my future wife. As a fisherman, I remember being struck by the confluence of all the different waters. Go back a few hundred years, I reckoned, and this must have been a marvelous fishery. Since my commute took me directly overhead, I had located and identified the Gowanus Canal, on the map an isolated penetration of blue into the borough. It was not far from my apartment, but at the time I didn't associate "urban" with "angling." Government intelligence. Jumbo shrimp. That sort of thing. Even if I had, the conditions of the inlet in those days would have put an end to any ideas about catching something live. Instead, I lamented that fishing was on hold indefinitely while I tried to approximate an adult and carve out a career.

Fast-forward to the present and offbeat angling. Sebastian and I have developed a greater consciousness about what makes us tick. Rather than stumbling across brown water, we're stalking it. I've reasoned, what more fetid hunting grounds than NYC. When I pass through the city now, be it on the FDR, BQE or GWB, I've got my eyes peeled. I see people casting *en masse* from piers. I've read about the successes around the Statue of Liberty. Fishing in the city seems reborn, maybe they should put commerce and industry on hold for a day and host a B.A.S.S. tournament in New York Harbor. It all comes as pleasant news but in a way, no surprise. Think about it. There are fish in the Atlantic, Jamaica Bay, the Hudson, Long Island Sound. Basically, all the surrounding bodies. The fish don't make out the skyline and turn tail. So at the least they're passing through during migration. As water conditions improve, there will be food present. The fish may even be able to see it. As maligned as the East River is, the punch line for water pollution since forever, it's all relative. By New York standards (and, in truth, more so all the time), "it ain't that bad." Maybe too good, I decide. There are browner waters to be found here. A real New Yorker's version of brown water.

Like the Newtown Creek. This tidal inlet starts at the East River and separates Brooklyn and Queens over much of its three-and-a-half mile length. I had crossed over it countless times on the mouthful Kosciuszko Bridge as I bounced up and down along the moonscape of the Brooklyn-Queens Expressway. I decide to take a closer look. Newtown Creek. Sounds harmless enough, like, "Honey, let's take the kids tubing on the Newtown Creek this weekend." Alas, their legs had disintegrated by day's end. Once home to over fifty oil refineries but nowadays too small for the big tankers, the creek is lined with the trappings of industry, both active and defunct, and is currently toxic beyond aquatic habitation. It's considered one of New York City's most polluted waterways. There's a perceptibly green hue, a liquid detergent look. It's not a reflection of the trees on the shore. There are few trees, and little shore. Just steel and concrete with a scattering of meager footholds for grass-roots efforts at reclamation. Fishing? Perhaps one day, but not yet. It would make for a great photo op, a bronze beauty silhouetted against the Manhattan skyline with a rusty oil tank in the foreground and some sludge on the water for texture. But you'd need a stunt fish.

The dismal results of my initial investigation bring a new problem to the surface. The offbeat angler gravitates to the fisheries seldom fished.

Up until now, that had included places that people either didn't know about, couldn't get to, or overlooked. Nowhere in New York City could be considered "remote," though access and navigation might prove challenging. The question that lingers is, are they overlooked and underfished, or just logically and purposely ignored. That is, if NYSDEC (New York State Department of Environmental Conservation) has scientifically determined that the water quality will not support life, then a journey into an estuary like Newtown Creek seems downright preposterous. I might as well be casting from a gargoyle off of the Chrysler Building.

The situation requires adding a layer of refinement to the Brown Water philosophy. A subtle but important distinction. The water has to have fish. Or at least the potential for fish. I sought extreme conditions and had found them, but this time I'd gone too far. The easiest solution would be to evacuate and head for bluer pastures. Wouldn't sleep too well if I did that. Or maybe stick around but drift over to the documented bounty around Liberty Island. Troll from the Staten Island Ferry. Nudge my way onto a pier along the Upper East Side. Under the broader theme of Offbeat Angling, all would seem to qualify. But somewhere deep inside I'm developing higher aspirations. These options, while enticing, are for a pseudo-New Yorker. The city is tough, and once again it's testing me.

My thoughts drift back to the halcyon days of my cattle-car commute over the Gowanus. I continue to have friends and relatives in and around the five boroughs, so I make some inquiries about the canal. The responses run the gamut, from a chuckle or a raised eyebrow to some tempered encouragement. My wife's uncle, Brooklyn-born and raised, offers the most colorful analysis, noting the Gowanus as a reputed Mafia disposal site and suggesting that if not careful I might be "sleepin' with the fishes" instead of hooking them. I dismiss the negativity and continue pushing the envelope with a second investigation.

The Gowanus Canal was originally a creek, so named by Dutch settlers in the 1600's for Chief Gowanee of the Canarsee tribe. At the time, it was a saltwater marshland thriving with wildlife, including oysters said by the natives to be "as big as a dinner plate." Farming grew and oyster harvests became Brooklyn's first export. In 1776, on the heels of a surprise attack from Staten Island, General Washington suffered a defeat at the hands of the British along the shores of the Gowanus. The canal was built during the Civil War as part of the city's attempt to improve navigation and accommodate commercial shippers, like the oyster farmers, as well as industrial users. Soon after, printing plants, oil-storage facilities and dye works sprang up, producing so much pollution that the waterway was nicknamed "Lavender Lake."

With limited tidal exchange, the pollution and unlimited discharge of raw sewage had transformed the mostly-stagnant waters into an open-air cesspool.

By the turn of the century unregulated industry was in full swing. At the time, manufactured gas, or the gasification of coal, was a popular fuel. Noxious fumes and toxic by-products like tar and benzene were emitted into air, soil and water from the dozens of gashouses that now bordered the canal. The area became known as the Gashouse District, today a term similar to "the wrong side of the tracks." In response to deteriorating conditions and mounting concerns, the city declared the situation a public health nuisance and set about to take corrective measures. In 1911 the flushing tunnel was built. One mile long and thirteen feet wide, the tunnel connected Buttermilk Channel (the section of the East River between Brooklyn and Governors Island, just south of the Brooklyn Bridge) to the head of the canal near Douglass Street, thus creating a continuous waterway. A massive ship's propeller was installed at a flushing station at the north end. The propeller was reversible and generated flow in either direction, enough to push the stagnant water out. Sort of like a giant toilet.

The concept worked and water conditions rapidly improved. Pollution still poured in, but now it had a place to go. By mid-century, however, the focus of waterfront industry had shifted to New Jersey. Many of the plants and factories on the canal lay abandoned. The Army Corps of Engineers, which had been supplementing the flush with regular dredging of the canal, ceased its efforts. In 1969, the propeller malfunctioned, broke, and remained that way for the next thirty years. Meanwhile, the canal returned to its former misery. The piers were still home to a number of industrial concerns, but low-income residential use was on the rise: sewage became the greater culprit. A new waste control facility in the neighboring Red Hook section promised help but, in wet weather especially, the plant proved inadequate. Once again the city recognized a dire need and, in 1999, repaired and reactivated the flushing station. As before, the water cleaned up and reports indicate encouraging dissolved oxygen levels and better salinity and clarity. This despite the ongoing contributions of over fifty CSOs (combined sewage outfalls) and a canal floor lined with at least twenty feet of fly ash (toxic sediment). Gravel yards, cement works, asphalt plants. Bottles, cans, diapers. Progress, maybe, but the punch list remains long.

With this kind of history and information in hand, you can imagine my enthusiasm at the thought of visiting such a garden spot. Not to mention that my vision of the modern canal environment is still blurry. How and where to gain access with the two-person kayak I have in

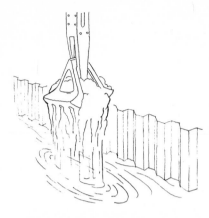

mind for the trip. Or whether that's a good idea at all. What's the chance for dangerous currents and extreme tides, or tankers, tugs and barges that might run me over? And always, there's that nagging toxicity issue. I wonder if my fly-fishing vest would fit over an astro-naut suit as I weigh how best to proceed. Then, lo and behold, I dis-cover that National Estuaries Day is coming up. How could I have for-gotten? A schedule of upcoming events in my latest copy of *New York* magazine mentions that the Gowanus Canal will be included in the celebration. It sounds like there's going to be a lot going on, although you never can tell when you read about an event like this. It could turn out to be me and the operator of the flushing station. But the coinci-dence seems providential, so I mark it down on my calendar.

On the eve of the big day I drive down to stay at my father-in-law's on Staten Island. Like his brother, born and raised in Brooklyn. A real New Yorker if ever there was one. Somehow he's been overlooked as a potential source of inside information on the canal, but when I pick his brain I find that the pickings are slim. And he doesn't know any-thing about the canal either. He didn't grow up near it and had spent his youth in the back of a bakery, at a time when kids actually con-tributed to the family income rather than drain it. He's up for a trip, though, and the next morning we cross the Verrazano Narrows through a foggy drizzle.

The home base for Estuaries '03 is the Carroll Street Bridge. We park a few blocks up and along the way pass Monte's, the first Italian restaurant in the borough and a New York institution, the former hangout for everyone from Al Capone to Frank Sinatra to the Brooklyn Dodgers starting nine. Pop-in-law offers that back in the day, the Miss Rheingold Beer competition was "unofficially" decided with a special audition in one of Monte's private rooms. At 8 a.m. it's closed of course and, sadly, we resort to a McDonald's around the corner for breakfast. Following that we report to the event site, in itself an inter-esting artifact. It's one of the few extant retractile bridges anywhere. Via a track and pulley system it *slides* diagonally backward to allow boat traffic to pass. A healthy turnout, all doubtless real New Yorkers, is waiting anxiously for the start of the day's festivities. Pops is gregari-ous to a fault and launches into immediate conversation with the morning's first victim, an estuarian septuagenarian who doesn't (or perhaps pretends not to) speak any English, but nods sufficiently. Meanwhile, I'm more interested in my physical surroundings, in particular a curious cylindrical structure across the water. Someone has retro-fitted a residence or studio of some kind into an old oil-storage drum. It's been dressed in stucco and has doors, windows, decks, and a conical asphalt roof with a ring of skylights. The surrounding property looks mostly like a vacant lot but with a geometric grid of newly-planted trees in the middle. At the far end, next to the canal, there's an automatic overhead door trimmed out with razor wire, a modern-day portcullis for this urban castle. But more intriguing still is the property's floating dock, complete with a small power boat (outfitted with a landing net, I notice) and better yet, a WaveRunner! The additional pollution aside, if someone is actually jet-skiing through the canal it can only be good news. Looking back across the water, I spy a jumping baitfish.

A number of canal-friendly groups have arrived with displays and information. The Brooklyn Center for the Urban Environment (BCUE) has organized and sponsored the event. Then there's Urban Divers, a stout-hearted brigade that regularly descends the murky depths (can they really see down there?). The Canal Dredgers Canoe Club has two crafts on standby at the nearby Second Street-End Park for today-only discount rides. Their very existence allays my kayaking fears. Red Dive, a performance art troupe, is four women clad in red jumpsuits (they really do look a lot like astronauts) playing their new Gowanus CD featuring interviews, music and sampled "canal sounds." The DEP and other municipal and state organizations are on hand as well. It's all very exciting and I'm genuinely impressed by the turnout and the level of support. And now the morning's centerpiece is arriving. The Chelsea Screamer, a water-taxi–presumably on loan from the Chelsea district of Manhattan–will be taking us on a guided boat trip. Pops and I and thirty or so others pile on and away we go. A group of seagulls bids us adieu.

At first, the scenery along the canal is pretty much as I expected, rust and rubble and decidedly bleak. Though brown water pursuits have broadened my horizons, I discover that my general mindset has remained stubbornly nestled in the wilderness beauty of the Yellowstone, the Hoh, the Housatonic and the numerous other immaculate waterways I've had the privilege of journeying. The guide interrupts his narrative, a blend of history and sightseeing, to point out an auspicious sign of nature returned.

"That's a cormorant. A diving bird that feeds on fish."

Precisely, I think, and when his buddies show up, there won't be any fish left. They'll march down the canal and systematically clean house, I've seen it done. Where I come from, the cormorant is about as appealing as a vulture and makes me want to take up hunting. Today, here, by himself, this one doesn't seem quite so threatening.

Whatever you make of it, there's a lot to see. It turns out the Carroll Street retractile is only the first in a series of civil engineering feats spanning the Gowanus. All the bridges open, yet no two in the same

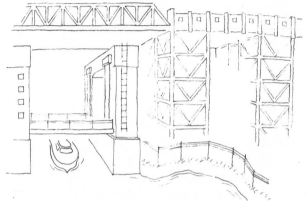

way. The Ninth Street Bridge, built directly under the F-train trestle, has elevator cables at four corners and actually hoists a segment of road straight up. But this one's higher to begin with and the Screamer slips underneath without holding up traffic. We're passing alongside the remnants of the past, like the infamous gashouses, but also witnessing the future. A Home Depot is up and running and a Lowe's is in the works not far away. McStores, they're everywhere, why not here. It comes as a surprise, my irritation at their arrival. Maybe I'm starting to warm up to the place. We stop not far from the Depot to check on an experimental oyster bed. It's doing okay.

The farther we go, the more things diversify. On the left, an asphalt plant that supplies roughly half of the paving material for the entire city. To the right, another street-end park; the energy from the neighborhood's collective efforts is palpable. Up ahead, an abandoned factory turned multi-use. An osprey sits atop the factory's pier.

"Blue Man Group rents space in there," notes the guide, and I imagine what the interior of that space might look like.

Out into Gowanus Bay and objects are getting bigger as the water widens. There's a battleship-grey tanker lying dormant, a boathand thinks it's actually resting on the bottom. Someone's taken an old freighter barge and converted it into a floating nightclub. Behind it looms a structure shaped like an inverted cone the size of a small mountain.

"This abandoned sugar refinery was recently purchased by Imelda Marcos. We suspect it may be filled with shoes," the guide quips as he gestures toward the cone. He's started working the room.

Past the refinery we can see a pair of brightly-colored grasshopper cranes. They're superhuman-scale and unload the container ships that stream into port each day. With Lower Manhattan towering directly opposite, they appear strangely contextual. I spot a pair of bait fishermen at nearby Valentino Pier.

While in the harbor, a biologist from BCUE tests the water for temperature, salinity and turbidity. Pops tries more than once to pronounce "turbidity" but gives up. Once back in the canal the tests are repeated. The results are remarkably similar, but the harbor is still ahead. The guide offers some irony, "The improving conditions have made life in the canal once again possible for a number of species, including a wood-borer worm that actually eats the docks."

The positive side is that the worm is a source of food for larger fish, along with the killies, minnows, mollusks, mussels, crabs and other creatures that have returned to the Gowanus. I suppose in the end it's the same old story: if there's food, they will come. But after all this I still don't have any definitive evidence. Back at Carroll Street and disembarking, I notice the owner of the oil-storage house at his dock, tending to his jet-ski.

"Ahoy there!" I yell over from the bridge, "That's quite a setup you've got. What do you know about fishing in here?"

"What do you want to know?" He's got better things to do than talk to a pseudo-New Yorker. I should have had Pops do my dirty work.

"Well, for starters, are there any fish?"

He gives me a patronizing smile. "There's no difference between here and the harbor. Or Jamaica Bay. Or Montauk Point, for that matter. Everything that's there, is in here."

He goes into further detail and adds that fish from polluted waters are every bit as edible as those found in the oceans. I'm not so sure about this last, especially when I'm holding a pregnancy warning pam-

phlet from Urban Divers entitled "Your Baby Eats the Fish You Eat!"
But I'm not looking to eat any fish anyway.

In fact, I'm not even looking to fish. Everything that's out there is in
here, I'm sure of it at this point. Stripers, blues, blackfish, fluke, flounder, porgies, the full cast of saltwater characters. Catching fish just isn't
that important today. The fish had been caught already, caught by the
canal as it made its triumphant return. That was the victory, and I was
fully satisfied. To test them now, even in catch-and-release fashion, was
not necessarily wrong but was decidedly anti-climactic. There would
be plenty of opportunity for that. My cynicism had given way, in a big
way, to the infectious enthusiasm that pervaded the Gowanus on
National Estuaries Day and probably most other days. This place was
amazing. These people were amazing. They had chosen to live in the
city, they didn't want to evacuate to find nature, and they didn't need
to. They were making do and doing quite well right here.

As for being a real New Yorker, I felt I had been given another
chance. A chance to realize what it really means. It has nothing to do
with a map of the subway, or logging hours at an address. Living at the
exact physical center of the city does not make you the most New
York of them all. In fact, being a New Yorker is not about living in
New York at all. It's a state of mind, the things you know or remember
about it, the people and places you love there, the ways it continues to
affect your life even when you're not there. This strange, single day
spent on a most improbable waterway had shown me that.

Pops suggests finding one of the access points and putting in, or just
fishing from a pier.

"Nah, I'm all set. Let's head to Joe and Pat's for a pie." We cross
back over the Verrazano and to a booth at the best pizzeria on Staten
Island and all of New York. And, therefore, probably the entire world.

A few months later, I get a call from Seb. He's thirsting for some
brown water and I have just the spot.

"Want to try out the Gowanus Canal?" I ask.

"Are you sure? Sounds a little intimidating."

"Don't worry, I'm a New Yorker."

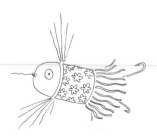

On Hallowed Ground

By Sebastian O'Kelly

Things are slow at work and, better yet, the boss is out swatting a little ball with a stick on some sylvan green expanse in the 'burbs. Plus, May was a busy, rainy month and I'm aching to wet a line. So that means it's time for me to pull my Clark Kent-Superman fishing routine. The mild mannered office worker turns into Superfisherman and heads to the nearest urban fishing blight during lunch hour and a half, with the taxicab serving as the transformational phone booth.

This time the stop is at 19th and Constitution Avenue on the Mall. I'll be checking out Constitutional Gardens, otherwise know as "the pond on the Mall" or "the pond by the Vietnam Veterans Memorial," a kidney-shaped body of water a couple acres in size, silt-filled and very shallow, maybe three or four feet at its deepest, with a nice paved path around it that is heavily used by tourists, joggers, and lunchers who work in the government buildings that line the other side of Constitution. I have heard that the Fish and Wildlife Service had stocked the pond last week for a kids event as part of National Fishing Week. I'm hoping for leftovers that the kids didn't get to.

Constitution Gardens may be best known as the temporary home for the so-called Tractor Man, a disgruntled tobacco farmer from North Carolina who drove his tractor into the water a couple of months ago and stayed there threatening to blow himself up unless the Federal government returned to the days of generous tobacco subsidies. It turns out, he was blowing smoke. The "organophosphate bombs" he told the cops he was carrying turned out to be nothing more than a couple of cans of Raid Roach and Flea Fogger bought at his local Wally World. He surrendered after three days of police stand-offs and blocks of barricaded streets.

I'm a little nervous as I walk down Constitution. Not that Tractor Man was about to re-appear anytime soon, given he was likely facing the first part of a long stay in the Big House. But with terrorism alerts a regular thing, a drawn out occupation of Iraq, and the Bush administration making homeland security a high priority, the notion of a guy pacing around a pond 1/4 mile from the White House with a rod tube in hand that, with a little imagination, could double as the casing for a rocket launcher, well, it's not too far off to see the authorities, M-16s drawn, descending en masse while I'm taking the rod out of the tube. Chris and I have been confronted by the constabulary while fishing in the past and the result has never been good. But a run in with the local county mounties is one thing, the thought of being confronted by the FBI, Secret Service, Bureau of Alcohol Tobacco and Firearms–the headquarters of each of which is within a one mile radius–has me feeling as exposed as a lone minnow in a school of hungry bass.

I comfort the willies by letting my over-active imagination wander. I pass several buildings where noted luminaries work and I ponder what they would think or say about my fishing excursion. First, I go by the National Academy of Sciences, home to some of the world's most brilliant academics. "Doctor, I believe your effort to identify the origin of the pine mezon is about as fruitless as that young man's quest to find fish in that muddy puddle." Next is the State Department, (in a high level meeting, North Korean official, No Nuk Havem, declares that his country "is no more likely to have nuclear weapons than that pond has fish." Then I pass the Federal Reserve. The stoic Alan Greenspan has called a meeting of his fellow pasty-faced Central Bankers. "I saw a man go fly fishing today on the Mall. It appears that disposable income and leisure time are both up. With the economy turning around, there will be no need to cut interest rates further."

At the Fed, I cut right through some trees to the pond. It is open space, per L'Enfant's vision, tucked in a bowl of rolling grassy banks with the National Monument looming high on the eastern side, with the western side lined by trees obscuring the entrance to the Vietnam

Veterans Memorial. A wide trail, paved in parts, graveled otherwise, hugs the shoreline. There is small, verdant island with a footbridge to it on the side nearest to Constitution. It looks like a good spot to eat lunch and start fishing. There are others eating on the island and a few children buzzing about. Quiet solitude on the Madison it is not. But since I've gotten on this urban fishing jag I'm used to having people around. I snarf down a ham sammie and Coke and rig up my rod with a small bonefish fly called a Crazy Charlie. A better option might be a "popcorn" fly or a "hot dog end" fly (tied with a yellow marabou plume to represent the critical mustard dab the fish hone in on) but this particular fly caught salmon for me in Alaska last summer so I figure, in a further ironic twist, it will work great here. Paradoxes almost always work in fishing. The water is shallow and the bottom muddy and not so fishy looking but I'm eager to cast. Across the way on the other side of the pond, I see another man fishing. With two partners in crime, this puts down my fears about getting patted down by the homeland security police and having my fishing forceps removed from my bag as a lethal weapon.

Unfortunately, after only a couple of casts, a large flotilla of ducks and geese come steaming toward me. Not only have I had to delicately avoid smearing my penny loafers with their carpet-bombed droppings spread across the grass, it appears that the birds have mistaken me as a source of food. Complicating matters further, several kids are zipping over, presumably to check out the geese. With no desire to get into the backing with a foul-hooked fowl or six-year-old, I reel up.

I try the bridge next. I have more room here. I search the water. There are several cattail clumps planted in underwater boxes that look promising. A couple of the boxes are empty, the plants hadn't taken

hold. I look closer at one nearby, just a foot under the surface. There is
a flicker of green. A largemouth is guarding the box, getting ready to
spawn, the box's pea gravel a perfect home for her prospective little
ones. I flip the fly in there, she explodes on it. But I'm jumpy and draw
the trigger too quick. The broody hen is now gun shy and spurns my
next two attempts. I spy a box further down and cast. There is a flash
of green, a flare of red gills, an opening of the jaw. Fish on! The bass
darts back and forth before coming to hand, a chunky fireplug of a fish
of maybe a foot. I quickly release her and she returns to her nest, a little irritated that a man has disturbed her from doing her thing, but
none the worse for wear otherwise. Over the next 15 minutes, I catch
several other bass scattered in the dozen boxes in the area.

A number of folks stop to watch and talk as I fish. This is something
I've grown to accept as part of the urban fishing experience. People are
naturally curious, if not a little bit startled, to see someone fishing in a
muddy pothole in the middle of a big city. Many of these folks walk by
these bodies of water day after day, never actually stopping to see if anything is in there. For someone who has spent most of his life flipping
over rocks, this lack of curiosity about the natural world, albeit immersed
in the most man-made setting, is puzzling. However, they become very
interested if you actually catch something. Then I usually get all sorts of
questions like, what is that fish, how did it get in here, what did you
catch it on, can you eat it and the occasional aren't you hurting the fish,
a dead giveaway as coming from some animal rights type, plus some
more studied questions, usually indicating a fellow fisherman possibly
weighing the notion of coming out here one day on his own. I generally
tolerate these questions with good humor. After all, I would be interested
too if walking by. Occasionally, someone gets in the way, hangs around
a little too long, or asks a stupid question like, how does the worm stay
on the hook when you are throwing the line back and forth like that.
But for the most part, people respect my space and prerogative.

One woman stops and asks me to show her where the fish are. I point to a bass fanning herself in a box. She can't hone in on where I'm pointing. I realize the average person spends more time looking at a dead fish on a plate than a live one under water. So they don't really know how to look, or what to look for. I try to guide her a little closer and tell her to watch for movement. After a minute, she finally spots the fish and a big grin comes across her face. She is very pleased with the discovery and I take satisfaction in having led her to it.

Not everyone notices or stops. A tourist couple goes past, their heads down and talking quietly. It's clear they've just been to the Vietnam Veterans Memorial, a moving experience as anyone who's been there will tell you, and not one you walk away from skipping and snapping your fingers. It's one of my favorite monuments on the Mall, though I hesitate to use such a word as it doesn't lend itself to the necessary gravity of that angled edifice with all those fallen soldiers whose names are inscribed on its smooth, glossy back surface.

Most know the history of the monument. Like the War itself, the process of siting and designing the Memorial was long, tortured and controversial until a 21-year-old Yale architecture student named Maya Lin stepped into the flame to create a simple design that has been the balm to heal the wounds that nearly rended our country in two. I think of walking over to visit but I decide not to. It is not a trip taken lightly after the whimsy of having danced around Constitutional Gardens with a fly rod in hand.

When Chris and I decided to write this book, I ran an Internet search to see if there were any other Brown Water Boys out there. Sure enough, we were not the first to assume the title. There was another group of Brown Water Boys, some of whose names are inscribed on that wall 100 yards from me, who engaged in work far more deadly than fishing. They served in Vietnam as part of the legendary Admiral Elmo Zumwalt's Brown Water Navy, running riverine reconnaissance and search and destroy missions in the Mekong Delta over 30 years ago. They did the dirty work, the sneak up in the dark, cut their throats, mine the harbor, then blend back into the terrain kind of work, the sort of stuff that has been lionized in so many films from serious classics like *Apocalypse Now* to the chop-chop flicks of Chuck Norris. Only these were real fellows who earned their name in places named "Blood Creek," "Coral Reef," "Rocket Alley," and "Killer Forest."

I wonder how many of the Brown Water Boys fished growing up. I'm sure a lot did. Some may even have brought their rods to Vietnam, hoping for an R & R day to have a go at a nearby rice paddy for some of those big carp and koi and the chance for a meal other than bland K rations. They probably discovered that carp over there are as difficult to fool as they are in the U.S., although with an M-16 on hand there is always a fall back option that would guarantee a meal of koi *fricasse* for the platoon.

I decide to head over to where the guy was fishing earlier. There are a couple of other guys fishing the same spot now. It's clearly a happening location and I'd like to find out why for future missions. I spot a bright orange koi out of casting range. It is scouting for food around what appears to be a sunken breadmaker, one of those in vogue appliances, post-expresso but pre-latte machine, from the 1990's that quickly faded from the mass culinary consciousness. A guy in a goatee passes me and says hi, then circles back.

"There's a good spot down there," he states, pointing his finger to where I'm heading.

"Yeah," I reply. "I've had good luck by the bridge."

"We've been slaying them by this pipe where they pump water in and out. The Fish and Wildlife service dumped 1,200 fish in here last week. Bass, carp, catfish. Even a few koi."

"Really? I knew there was a kids' event going on as part of National Fishing Week."

He nods his head. "The kids were nailing them. I caught a koi that day on a Borski's Slider (another type of bonefish fly). Busted my 5 weight."

I catch a glimpse of fishing madness in his eyes. I've been there and can spot it instantly in others. I introduce myself and he gives me a "seen you before glance." It turns out we sort of do know each other as cyberfriends on the tidalfish.com bulletin boards, Tony as One More Cast and I as Tissy Furnes (a childhood nickname whose genesis would take too long to explain here). We reach his friends and Tony makes the introductions. They are fishing on spin with a rubber worm and seem to be picking up a fish every fourth cast or so.

"I can see this is a hot spot." I stand to the side. It's their spot and I don't want to intrude unless invited to.

Tony points to the water. "It's a little deeper here. There's about a four-foot channel that runs out from the pipe. You see the fry over here. It's rocky too and everything is attracted to the water flow." He raises his hand. "Out in the middle, Fish and Wildlife sunk a couple of brush piles." He's now casting the rod and sets the hook on a small bass.

"I don't suppose you can wade out there?"

"Naw. I brought my waders last week. But I don't think they want people to get the idea they can swim in here. We've been fishing every lunch this week. Work is just a five minute walk away." Two of them work in IT for a high-end law firm while the third is one of the partner's kids.

"Has Fish and Wildlife given you guys any trouble about fishing here?"

One of Tony's buddies shakes his head. "They're psyched we are fishing. They want folks to take advantage of it."

"They're going to throw down some rubber mats," Tony adds.

"Rubber mats?"

"Yeah. Like Astroturf. They use it as a base for plants. They really want to build a year-round fishery. Some of these bass survive year to year but not in significant numbers. The regional guy for Fish and Wildlife told me that there were five-pound bass in here a long time ago. They'd like to get back to that."

"That's cool," I remark.

"Here," Tony says, generously stepping aside. "Take a shot. Bet you get one first cast. They haven't seen a fly yet today."

As predicted, I hook and land a bass on my first toss. Grins all round. The two of us alternate a few more casts, but we get no more takes. That's O.K. – I've seen enough to know this is a spot worth coming back to. I look at my watch. It has indeed been a long lunch and while I suspect the boss is still out on the course doing his best to stay under triple figures, it is always conceivable that he could call in from the 18th green. We exchange goodbyes and I head back up to Constitution.

As I trudge along, my mind drifts back to those original Brown Water Boys. I hope they don't mind, those listed on the wall and the others who are still among the living, that Chris and I have ex-appro-priated their *nom de plume*. Our use of it is certainly less valorous and if there was some sort of central address to write for permission, I would. But there is none and now that I give it second thought most of the BWBs I'm sure wouldn't care and might even get a kick out of it, the fact that I'm here fishing in this soon-to-be restored urban ecosystem, not but a block away from hallowed ground that is rightly reserved for them.

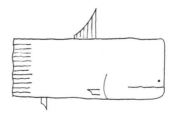